"Our LIF … ake it."

… s Aurelius

THO … TS TO BUILD ON

BY M. R. KOPMEYER

America's Success Counselor To Millions

This is a book of THOUGHTS to build your LIFE on. It is a unique book . . . 80 entirely different and unrelated chapters . . . each providing about 10 minutes of stimulating and rewarding reading . . . each starting your *own* thoughts on a positive course of immediately useful and profitable ideas . . . so that you thus may build your life as *you* want it.

It is the purpose of this book to stimulate constructive thoughts, to give your thoughts improved direction and greater substance, to provide the kind of motivational thinking *which will enable you to deal successfully with people and problems.*

UBSPD

UBS Publishers Distributors Ltd.

New Delhi • Bangalore • Chennai

Calcutta • Patna • Kanpur

UBS Publishers' Distributors Ltd.
5 Ansari Road, New Delhi-110 002
Phones: 3273601, 3266646 • *Cable*: ALLBOOKS •
Fax: 3276593, 3274261 • e-mail: ubspd@gobookshopping.com
10 First Main Road, Gandhi Nagar, Bangalore-560 009
Phones: 2263901, 2263902, 2253903 • *Cable*: ALLBOOKS •
Fax: 2263904 • e-mail: ubspd.bng@bgl.vsnl.net.in
6, Sivaganga Road, Nungambakkam, Chennai-600 034
Phones : 8276355, 8270189 • *Cable* : UBSIPUB • *Fax* : 8278920
e-mail: ubspd.che@md4.vsnl.net.in
8/1-B, Chowringhee Lane, Calcutta-700 016
Phones: 2441821, 2442910, 2449473 • *Cable*: UBSIPUBS •
Fax : 2450027 • e-mail: ubspdcal@cal.vsnl.net.in
5 A, Rajendra Nagar, Patna-800 016
Phones: 672856, 673973, 686170 • *Cable* : UBSPUB • *Fax*: 686169
e-mail: ubspdpat@dte2.vsnl.net.in
80, Noronha Road, Cantonment, Kanpur-208 004
Phones : 369124, 362665, 357488 • *Fax* : 315122
e-mail: ubskup@lw1.vsnl.net.in

Distributors for Western India:
M/s Preface Books
Unit No. 223, (2nd floor), Cama Industrial Estate,
Sun Mill Compound, Lower Parel (W), Mumbai-400 013
Phones : 022-4988054 • *Telefax*: 022-4988048 •
E-mail: Oreface @ vsnl.com

Overseas Contact
475 North Circular Road, Neasden, London NW2 7QG, U.K.
Tele : (020) 8450-8667 • *Fax* : (020) 8452 6612 Attn: UBS

Reprint 2001

Printed at Ram Printograph, Delhi (India)

×+

When You Bought This Book, You Bought Stock In Yourself!

The best investment you can make is in YOU.

You can make more money or acquire more of whatever you want—by investing in YOU than in any other investment.

When you bought this book, you bought stock in YOURSELF.

Nobody buys stock in anything unless he or she has *confidence* in it. Because, in buying this book, you really bought stock in YOURSELF, you have proved that you have *confidence* in YOURSELF.

Now that you have bought stock in YOURSELF and proved that you have *confidence* in YOURSELF, you have taken the first step in getting *whatever you want in life*.

This book now will tell you *how* to do it.

×+

YOURSELF STOCK CERTIFICATE

This certifies that you own

1,000,000 shares

of

STOCK IN YOURSELF

This is your certificate of confidence in yourself and your agreement to begin at once and constantly use proven success methods to get whatever you want as a worthy life goal.

Introduction

THOUGHTS ... The Building Blocks of Life

This is a book of THOUGHTS TO BUILD ON.

Why?

Because with our THOUGHTS we build our personalities, our characters, our lives.

Our THOUGHTS determine what we *are* and what we *will be* throughout the future. *All* great religions, *all* great philosophies, *all* great thinkers, *all* great achievers, affirm that we actually *are* the materialization of our THOUGHTS.

The Bible says, "As a man THINKETH, so *is* he."

Buddha taught, "*All* (yes, *all*) that we *are* is the result of what we have THOUGHT."

Wrote the great emperor and philosopher of ancient Rome, Marcus Aurelius, "Our LIFE is what our THOUGHTS make it."

Eighteen centuries later, the eminent psychologist-philosopher William James, reaffirmed, "Belief (confident THOUGHT) creates the *actual fact*."

The American educator, Amos Bronson Alcott, taught, "THOUGHT means LIFE, since those who do not

THINK do not live in any high or real sense. THINKING MAKES THE MAN."

So we learn from these great sources of wisdom throughout the ages that our THOUGHTS build our lives and in a very real sense our THOUGHTS ARE OUR LIVES.

THOUGHTS are the building blocks of our lives and thoughts build upon themselves, for as George Sala wrote, "Thought engenders thought . . . the more you think, the better you will express yourself."

THOUGHTS are the building blocks of PERSONAL POWER.

Emerson states categorically, "THOUGHTS rule the world."

Clergyman William Ellery Channing wrote, "Secret study, silent THOUGHT, is the mightiest agent in human affairs. What a man does outwardly is but the expression and completion of his inward THOUGHT."

Henrich Heine, the much-quoted German poet, turned to concise prose to make it clear that, "The men of action are, after all, only the unconscious instruments of the men of THOUGHT."

And back to Emerson, who deeply believed in the power-force of THOUGHT, "There is no THOUGHT in any mind, but it quickly tends to convert itself into a *power*.

Jonathan Edwards emphasized it, "The ideas and images (THOUGHTS) in men's minds are the invisible *powers* that constantly govern them."

Then, in addition to providing the building blocks of life, and in addition to being the root-source of personal power we find that it is THOUGHT by which we attain *personal success.*

The world-famous, preacher-psychologist-writer, Dr. Norman Vincent Peale says, "THINK success, visualize success, and you will set in motion the power force of the realizable wish. When the mental picture (THOUGHT) or attitude is strongly enough held, it actually seems to control conditions and circumstances."

Dr. Walter Scott, famous psychologist and president of Northwestern University taught, "Success or failure in business is caused more by mental (THOUGHT) attitudes than by mental capacities."

Disraeli, "Nurture your mind with great THOUGHTS; to believe in the heroic makes heroes."

And clergyman John William Teal, "It is the habitual THOUGHT which frames itself into our life. Our confidential friends have not so much to do in shaping our lives as THOUGHTS have which we harbor."

Isaac Taylor, "THINKING, not growth, makes manhood."

Johann Pestalozzi, the Swiss educator, taught, "Man, by THINKING only becomes truly man. Take away THOUGHT from man's life, and what remains?"

Confucius, "Learning without THOUGHT, is labor lost."

And Emerson, once again, "No accomplishment, no assistance, no training, can compensate for lack of belief (confident THOUGHT)."

Then, Henry Ford, "Whether you THINK you can or THINK you can't—you are right."

So . . . our THOUGHTS determine what we *are* and what we *will* be; our THOUGHTS are our source of personal *power;* our THOUGHTS are the principal means of our *successful achievement,* and reveal it as William Plumer said, "THOUGHTS, even more than overt acts, reveal character."

And, as if all that were not enough, THOUGHTS can bestow upon us the gifts of *happiness* and *pleasures.*

From the ancient wisdom of Marcus Antoninus, "The HAPPINESS of your life depends upon the quality of your THOUGHTS."

Are you lonely? Sir Sidney wrote, "They are never alone who are accompanied by *pleasant* THOUGHTS."

Bishop John Williams advised, "Garner up *pleasant* THOUGHTS in your mind, for *pleasant* THOUGHTS make *pleasant lives.*"

Another clergyman, Charles Hadden Spurgeon, used to preach that, "Good THOUGHTS are blessed guests and should be heartily welcomed."

And Robert South taught that, "Nothing is comparable to the *pleasure* of an active and prevailing THOUGHT."

But, perhaps, the pleasure of THINKING was best expressed by the wise and much-quoted lawyer of another generation, John Foster, who wrote, "The *pleasantest* things in the world are *pleasant* THOUGHTS, and the greatest art in life is to have as many of them as possible."

And so, having focused the wisdom of the great minds of many centuries on the power, the benefits and pleasures of THOUGHT, let us explore, in the chapters that follow, THOUGHTS TO BUILD ON—*now*—in the exciting, confusing, threatening, sometimes happy, but always wonderful, world in which we live.

Thousands of years of wisdom, experience and observation have proven, beyond any doubt, that YOU WILL BECOME WHAT YOU THINK.

So . . . what *should* you think?

If you let your mind drift, it will idly contemplate whatever happens to attract its attention and will set in motion a chain of thoughts, one leading to another to no telling where! Then something else will attract its attention and the first chain of thoughts will be broken by another undirectional chain.

Therefore this book: "THOUGHTS TO BUILD ON." Its purpose is to give your thoughts direction and substance—to channel your thoughts toward rewarding ends.

But this book will not do your thinking for you . . . because you will *become* only what *you,* yourself, THINK. Therefore, this is a very unique book. Each brief chapter (and there are eighty) can be read in just several minutes. Each chapter gives you a different, stimulating

THOUGHT TO BUILD ON . . . then sets you free . . . to pass it by . . . or to think about it as deeply and as long as you wish.

You may return to the stimulating thought-starter in each chapter as often as you wish—but return to it you must, because it will not be repeated, and each following chapter will contain an entirely *different* thought! Each and every chapter contains the stimulus of an interesting, exciting, different thought which is totally unrelated in context, if not entirely in substance, to all preceding and following chapters and thoughts.

So you can read this book forward, backward, start in the middle or anywhere. Glance down the table of "Contents" and choose the thoughts you wish to think about at the moment. You can spend a few minutes with this book . . . or an hour . . . or an evening.

It will fill the brief, empty spaces of your spare time . . . while you are commuting, waiting, or just relaxing.

In any case, you will find it interesting, stimulating, helpful. It will give you an unlimited variety of THOUGHTS TO BUILD ON . . . and give you plenty of room to do your own thinking.

For . . . "As a man THINKETH—so IS he."

THOUGHTS TO BUILD ON

Contents

The 80 thought-stimulating chapters which will build a more successful YOU!

Chapter 1

Stand Tall

One of the most important . . . most helpful . . . most rewarding . . . lessons I have learned in a rather long and eventful life can be described in just two words: STAND TALL!

By urging you to *stand tall,* I don't mean merely to stand erect, although that's part of it. I mean that you should *heighten your entire personality* by standing tall in three ways:

(1) STAND TALL . . . PHYSICALLY
(2) STAND TALL . . . MENTALLY
(3) STAND TALL . . . SPIRITUALLY

When you *stand tall* in all three parts of your total personality, you attain a *total* stature which puts you in command of life's situations. You stride gracefully, easily, through life with an inner and outer calmness which expresses your self-confidence and your assured capability of coping with whatever conditions you may meet along the way.

I can give you no better prescription for traveling through life boldly and successfully than this—and I shall give it to you in sufficient detail that you never again will bow to man nor to circumstance. So let's begin . . .

(1) STAND TALL . . . PHYSICALLY

There's an art to this, but it is an art which is easily learned. When you learn it, you will feel a high sense of exhilaration and a bold firmness of command.

First, you begin simply by standing erect. Not slouched. Not slumped. Not stooped. But not stiff nor tense, either. Just erect. Then you calmly *s-t-r-e-t-c-h* upward, concentrating entirely on reaching higher with the top of your head. That's all—just lift yourself with the top of your head. Do not strain—easily *l-i-f-t* so that you can feel that the top of your head is lifting your weight off your feet so that you "stand lightly", almost weightlessly.

When you walk, walk lightly. No plodding. No stomping. And no timid toddling, either. Just stride lightly, with an easy glide, your legs swinging smoothly back and forth like pendulums.

Don't stretch your shoulders upward. Don't pull your shoulders backward. Just *relax* them. You control the position of your shoulders with your chest. Yes, that's right, you control the position of your shoulders with your chest. Expand your chest. Push your chest forward and upward. *Lead with your chest!*

Don't lift your chin (that will make you look arrogant and egotistical). Just keep your chin firm and level. Do *all* your "lifting" with the *top* of your *head.* But remember, do it naturally, easily. Don't strain. Don't be tense. Keep relaxed . . . poised . . . balanced . . . buoyant . . . light . . . *standing and walking on air!*

You will be amazed at how *standing tall—physically*—will immediately improve your personality, your poise, your self-confidence, your attitude toward others and your zest for life. You will instantly notice the gratifying reaction of others to your improved attitude of confidence, presence and command.

Standing tall—physically—will take years off the appearance of older people. A characteristic of old age is the curved back, the stooped shoulders drooping forward, the slumped figure. Yet this most obvious sign of increasing years and increasing physical deterioration will *vanish instantly* when an older person *stands tall—physically*—by following the simple directions in the preceding paragraphs. The health value alone is worth many times the effort (if any) required to form this beneficial habit of youthful posture. The nerves are no longer pinched, the muscles are no longer cramped, the blood flows freely, and chest is expanded to greatly increase the intake of stimulating oxygen.

Older people who *stand tall—physically*—not only look years younger . . . they feel years younger!

But, no matter what your age, *standing tall—physically*—is just the beginning of this easy way to heighten your personality. Frequently re-read the foregoing instructions. Constantly practice them until you have made them a natural part of your life.

Then you are ready for the second step:

(2) STAND TALL . . . MENTALLY

There's an old, but tried and true slogan which says, "Always go first class." I want to add an equally important slogan, "*Always think first class!*" Don't clutter up your mind with second class thoughts. It is just as easy to think *big* as it is to think small. And remember, you actually become the sum-total of your thoughts. "As a man thinketh in his heart (deeply believes) so *is* he." You can become no bigger, no better, no finer, no more successful than your dominant thoughts. So think *big! Stand tall . . . mentally!*

Life isn't going to give you more than you ask. Employment managers say that almost all job-applicants apply for low-paying jobs. Only a few apply for jobs paying better wages. Almost no one applies for the high-salaried jobs! Almost no one thinks *big!* So if you want to be a standout in the crowd, if you want to be looked *up* to . . . *stand tall . . . mentally.*

Your thoughts are the fuel for achievement. You wouldn't start out each morning by putting a handful of dirt into the fuel-tank of your car. Then don't stall the mechanism of your mind by dumping in thoughts of fear, anger, hatred, jealousy or guilt. Don't let little thoughts make you little, too.

Don't get stuck with the present. No matter how insignificant your present is—*think big about your future.* Think creatively. Think: "How can I improve?" (*Add value.*) Think: "How can I do more?" (*Add quantity.*) Learn—add facts. You can't build *anything* unless you have the materials. You can't build something out of nothing. So learn! Use what you learn to think *big!* Then you'll *stand tall . . . mentally.* And you will be amazed at the immediate improvement in your attitude toward life . . . and the admiration of others for you.

Then, there's the third way to heighten your personality. It is:

(3) STAND TALL . . . SPIRITUALLY

No person really stands tall in the judgment of his fellow men or even in the constant scrutiny of his own conscience unless he is too big spiritually to be little morally. There is a lift in *standing tall—spiritually—*which cannot be achieved in any other way. Yet, paradoxically, while it lifts you up, it also gives you that calm firmness which makes you impregnable to the vicissitudes of life.

If you have not achieved that spiritual height, if you cannot stand that tall spiritually—your God is too small!

It is only when you can accept INFINITY . . . boundless without dimension . . . timeless throughout eternity . . . holy beyond reverence . . . and know that you, in some spiritual way, are a part of it . . . only then can you really *stand tall . . . spiritually.*

And, *that* will make all the difference!

So . . . if you would live Life to the fullest . . . *stand tall!*

(1) STAND TALL . . . PHYSICALLY . . .
to achieve confidence!

(2) STAND TALL . . . MENTALLY . . .
to attain wisdom!

(3) STAND TALL . . . SPIRITUALLY . . .
to be triumphant!

Chapter 2

Divide And Conquer

Constantly we are reminded that it is the subtle or overt objective of our enemies to "*divide and conquer*".

Certainly an alliance, a nation, an organization —if it can be sufficiently divided—loses its will to win, and, in its confusion and dissension, loses its ability to survive.

There is no doubt about the effectiveness of the principle: "Divide and conquer." So let's apply it to *you.*

In fact, let's apply the principle of "divide and conquer" to you in the following two most important fields:

(1) Your personal HEALTH: physical, mental and emotional.

(2) Your SUCCESS in life.

Let's start with (1) Your HEALTH. Surely by now everybody is familiar with Dr. William Osler's famous prescription to: "Live one day at a time." He wisely said: "The load of tomorrow, added to that of yesterday, carried today, makes the strongest falter." And so it does.

Overburdening, by trying to carry too many loads all at once, will crush you physically, destroy you mentally and wreck you emotionally.

Yet most people carry the "load of *tomorrow*" in their imaginations: "What will I do about that" . . . "Suppose this should happen?" . . . "When will I find time to do so many things? . . . see so many people? . . . go so many places?'" And so on and on.

They "live out" in their imaginations today—all the work they are going to do tomorrow. Thus they add tomorrow's work-load to today's work-load. And not only tomorrow's, but the day after, and the day after.

Then they do *yesterday's* work all over again today. "Suppose I had said this instead of that?" . . . "Perhaps, if I had just done it differently." . . . "Why didn't I think of it then?" . . . And again, on and on.

They re-do all of yesterday's work today and add this burden to the imagined burden of tomorrow's work. And not only yesterday's work, but usually the work of the day before that . . . and the day before that.

But they *must* do *today's* work—when they are already mentally re-doing the work of countless yesterdays and living, in their imaginations, the work and dangers of countless tomorrows. No wonder men and women break under the strain!

No wonder Dr. William Osler prescribed: "Live only *one* day at a time . . . live *today!*"

Divide and conquer!

Divide your life, as Dr. Osler recommended, into one-day compartments. Shut out all yesterdays. Shut out all tomorrows. Live only this one day: *today!* Then you have only *one* day's problems to conquer. And anybody can conquer just *one* day's problems!

Ask Alcoholics Anonymous. This highly successful organization teaches: "Do not decide to stop drinking forever. Just decide you will not take a drink *today.*" Not forever. Just *one* day. Divide and conquer!

Ask Robert Louis Stevenson. He wrote: "Anyone can carry his burden, however hard, until nightfall. Anyone can do his work, however hard, for one day. Anyone can live sweetly, patiently, lovingly, purely, for twenty-four hours."

Then begin to *divide* even more—so that you can *conquer* more!

Divide each day into the individual *tasks* to be done. Then concentrate on the task you are doing *now.* And *only* that task . . . the one you are doing right *now!*

Think not about the tasks just completed. Take the advice of psychologist William James: "When your decision is made and put into action—dismiss absolutely all care or responsibility about the outcome."

Think not about the tasks yet to be done. Let them come each in its time—not rushing at you all together like an avalanche—but coming in single file, unhurriedly, like the individual grains of sand dropping through an hourglass.

Thus you *divide*, into separate tasks, your daily work, and in so doing, *conquer* it.

Thus you achieve calmness, poise, tranquility.

And (2) SUCCESS!

Success—because you are able (physically, mentally and emotionally) to work with that easy, calm sureness which comes with concentrating solely on the job at hand.

Your mind is not cluttered with yesterday's, or tomorrow's, or even with today's other tasks. It is free to search the whole broad field of thought for the best solution of each problem in turn, and, being undistracted, to find it quickly, surely.

This is the way of success. It has always been the way of great thinkers and great achievers. It is the "great quietness" which is the source of clear thought and calm power.

Strange, that so many people have not thought of this before. Everybody knows about "divide and conquer"—yet how few apply this success technique to their own lives . . . to their own daily tasks.

And yet, if just they would "divide and conquer"—first their days—then their tasks—they would no longer be average people. They would take upon themselves the majesty of serenity, the calm sureness of concentration—and the inevitability of success.

Chapter 3

How To Learn From A Guided Missle

Because man developed the intelligence to construct a guided missile, he should have the intelligence to learn from it.

A guided missile has a built-in mechanism which is a "homing" device to the target. When the missile gets even slightly off course—makes an error in direction—as is frequently the case, its guidance system makes the corrections necessary to get it back on course so that it will hit the target.

We should also note here that the missile cannot correct its course while it is standing still. It can only correct its errors when it is moving forward toward its target.

Now, what can you learn from the guided missile? You can learn these valuable lessons which will be of great benefit to you throughout all your life:

(1) You should have a target or, as the psychologists say, you should be "goal-oriented". You should have some specific objective in life and head directly for it.

(2) While you are moving toward your goal, you will make frequent errors, even as a guided missile does.

(3) You must learn to recognize these errors and acknowledge that they are errors. Otherwise you will not know that a correction is needed.

(4) Having recognized and admitted that you have made an error which would cause you to miss your goal, you simply correct it and get back on target. Note that you are no more embarrased or ashamed of the error than the missile is. Making, recognizing, admitting and correcting errors is simply the method of moving toward and accurately reaching any goal—a missile's goal or your life's goal.

Neither missiles nor people go directly to their goals in a straight line. Neither missiles nor people are that perfect—nor do they need to be. That's why they have built-in guidance systems.

You know, of course, about the guidance systems of missiles. At least you know that they have them and that it is the function of these guidance systems to recognize and correct the errors which the missiles inevitably make as they proceed to their targets.

How much do you know about your own personal guidance system?

Do you have a target, a goal in life? Are you

aiming at just ONE main goal? Think how confused and ineffective your personal guidance system would be if it tried to guide you to a number of goals in different directions! That's why the one-goal person reaches his goal quickly and effectively, while the person who tries to accomplish too many things simultaneously (instead of one at a time) zigzags his way futilely through life.

Do you keep moving forward toward your goal? Your personal guidance system cannot correct the direction in which you are moving—if you are *not* moving. So keep moving. Don't stop. Don't hesitate for fear of making an error. You can correct your error while you are moving forward. Life is like riding a bicycle. You can easily correct your direction while you are moving, but if you stop, you lose your balance, become shaky and fall.

You must expect to make errors and therefore constantly watch for them so you can correct them promptly. The more promptly you correct an error, the less you will have strayed off course and the more quickly you can get back on target.

Since you will accept errors as at natural part of life, you will not be ashamed of them, but simply accept them as something to be corrected on your way to your goal.

Your natural acceptance of errors, your not being embarrassed or ashamed of them, will free you forever from a "sense of guilt" and its accompanying mental and emotional anguish.

Of course, when you accept errors as a part of life, you must at the same time accept the fact that you have a personal guidance system which will correct your errors and head you directly to your one main goal.

How do you set your guidance system so that it will keep you on course to your goal? Here's how:

(a) Your personal guidance system is like a computer. You "feed" the details of your goal directly into the "memory" of your computer (which is your subconscious mind) and thus your guidance system knows, and never forgets for one second, exactly what your goal is.

(b) Once your guidance system is absolutely sure of what your one main goal is, it will guide you directly to it. You do not need to tell it how (even if you know). Your guidance system—subconscious mind—is a part of the Universal Mind which guides and operates everything from your own heartbeat to the movement of the planets. It is quite capable of guiding you to your goal and will easily do so.

(c) All you personally do is follow and co-operate with your guidance system. You will "know" what to do. You will be "given" the ability and power to reach your goal. Just relax, let your subconscious mind guide you—and move surely and confidently forward.

Thus man, who put the guidance systems in missiles, has discovered that he has had a personal guidance system within himself all the time! And, by constantly visualizing a "mental picture" of his goal, his personal guidance system will take him to it.

Chapter 4

How To Handle Unpleasantness And Solve Problems

Let's face it, there's a lot of unpleasantness in this old world of ours.

There are unpleasant conditions. There are unpleasant situations. And there are quite a few unpleasant people (although sometimes they are not as unpleasant as at others).

The optimist who cheerfully assures us that: "Life is just a bowl of cherries", neglects to add that some of the cherries may be sour.

Marcus Aurelius, one of the wisest rulers of the Roman Empire, wrote in his diary: "I am going to meet people today who talk too much, people who are selfish, egotistical, ungrateful. But I won't be surprised or disturbed, for I couldn't imagine a world without such people."

How shall we handle these unpleasant conditions, situations and people?

They fall into two general classifications with all sorts of variations in between. We shall consider only the two extremes and let the handling of variations follow the solutions of the major classifications.

First, there are the unpleasant conditions, situations and people about which little or nothing constructive can be done. Of course, something probably can be attempted about almost anything. But it often isn't worth the effort. Just because you are not getting anywhere by butting your head against a stone wall is no reason to increase your efforts and butt your head against the same stone wall even harder.

There are those who will exhort you to persist in overcoming all obstacles, to achieve your goal no matter what the cost. I suggest that it is more intelligent and productive to reach a sound judgment concerning how—or even *if*—you will proceed in a certain endeavor. It could well be that the same amount of effort might produce much more results if directed to other objectives.

So let us assume that you are involved in an unpleasant condition or situation, or with an unpleasant person, and you have decided that nothing constructive can or should be done. That does not cause the unpleasantness to vanish. It still remains, and, for your own peace of mind, you will have to deal with it.

Here's how:

First, take the wise advice of William James of Harvard, the father of applied psychology, who taught his students, "Be willing to have it so. Acceptance of what has happened is the first step in overcoming the consequences of any misfortune." And let me add: that advice includes acceptance of what now is happening (and cannot reasonably be prevented), and also what may be expected inevitably to happen in the future. Be willing to have it so. Don't fight it—if you can't beat it—ACCEPT it! Be willing to have it so. Then *adjust*. When Fate closes one door, Faith opens another. Seek the *open* door!

Now let's consider the other kind of unpleasantness which is a problem that can and must be solved. The following method is positively effective in solving all kinds of problems, not just unpleasant ones.

It might be well to mention here that most problems, as such, are not unpleasant, but primarily are stimulating. Certainly that should be your attitude toward all problems. For very many years, before I retired, I was president of a multi-million-dollar advertising agency. We used what we called the "Problem Approach Method" in working for 102 clients. That simply means that we approached every situation assigned to us as a problem to be solved. Naturally, we made a continuous study of all the best methods of solving problems.

Here, in condensed form, is the most effective method of solving problems:

(1) WRITE DOWN EXACTLY WHAT THE PROBLEM IS. Don't just think about it. Write it down. Write it down exactly, precisely, concisely. Remember that Charles Kettering, the great inventive genius of

General Motors, said, "A problem well stated is a problem half solved."

(2) WRITE DOWN EXACTLY WHAT ARE THE CAUSES OF THE PROBLEM. Get the facts. Get ALL the facts. Be sure the facts are exact, clear, objective and impartial—not selected to bolster some preconceived opinion. Especially, if you do have a preconceived opinion, be sure that you get all the facts that do NOT support your pre-judgment, as well as those which do. Herbert Hawkes of Columbia University taught, "Half the worry in the world is caused by people trying to make decisions before they have sufficient knowledge on which to base a decision. If a man will devote his time to securing knowledge in an impartial, objective way, his worries will usually evaporate in the light of knowledge." So get the facts. Be sure you know the exact causes of the problem before you try to solve it.

(3) WRITE DOWN EVERY POSSIBLE EFFECTIVE SOLUTION. Be sure each possible solution of your problem is the impartial result of "trying the case" from both sides by first pretending you are the lawyer trying the case FOR the solution, then imagining you are the lawyer trying the case AGAINST the solution. Then if the solution still appears to be effective, include it in your list.

(4) DECIDE DEFINITELY WHICH SOLUTION TO PUT INTO EFFECT. If you have carefully analyzed the pros and cons of each solution as recommended in the preceding paragraph (3), then your

final decision should be relatively easy. If it still is difficult to decide, and if you have time, feed all of your possible solutions into your "mental computer" (subconscious mind) and let it work on the solutions in its own way for the next few days and nights. Meanwhile relax. The best solution will soon become clear and definite in your mind. Then decide that THAT is your best solution and that you will put it into effect, forgetting all others.

(5) START IMMEDIATELY TO PUT THAT SOLUTION INTO EFFECT AND PERSIST VIGOROUSLY. All the previous steps will get you nowhere unless they end in immediate, definite and vigorous *action*. And when once you begin to act, don't look back over your shoulder. Go right ahead; see it through. You'll never get better instructions than from famous William James, who taught, "When once a decision is reached and execution is the order of the day, dismiss aboslutely all responsibility and care (anxiety) about the outcome." If you have conscientiously put into effect all of the preceding five steps in this Problem Solving Method, you can be sure the outcome will be very satisfactory.

To know how to effectively handle the inevitable unpleasant conditions, situations and people which are a part of every life and to be able to successfully solve the problems which constantly come your way, will make you master of most of life's difficulties. That knowledge now is in your hands.

Chapter 5

Can You Separate Facts From Opinions?

I could see the lines of worry and fear etching themselves ever more deeply in the face of the past-middle-aged man who told me, "I've lost my fortune through unwise investments. It's too late to start over. My family and I will live out our lives in disgrace and poverty."

This man had only *one fact*. All of the rest of his statement was *opinion.*

Accepting your *opinions* as being *facts* can ruin you!

What was this man's one fact? It was a *fact* that he had lost a sizable fortune through unwise investments.

It was merely *his own opinion* that, being past middle-age, it was too late to start over and build another fortune.

It was merely *his own opinion* that he and his

family would have to live out their lives in disgrace and poverty.

But by taking just one fact and magnifying it by adding a number of opinions (which are not facts) you can reach conclusions which are so wrong that they can do great damage.

Let's take the case of the middle-aged "failure" just described.

We'll start with his *one fact:* he had lost his money through unwise investments. Well, maybe that was stupid. Perhaps with more caution and better advice the loss could have been avoided. But certainly it was neither original nor unusual. Often men who amass large fortunes lose substantial sums of money from time to time. They accept their losses as part of the business of fortune-making.

Many men have made and lost a number of fortunes. Almost all of them have recouped their losses and greatly increased their wealth. There is a state of mind and a technique of fortune-making.

So even the *fact* that our friend did lose his money was no cause for panic. Surely it was no cause for him to compound his misfortune by adding adverse *opinions* which were not even facts.

Now, let's have a look at his *own opinions* which he mistook to be facts and which caused his desperation and his hesitation to vigorously work his way back to the top.

(1) "It's too late to start over." That, of course, was merely *his opinion.* It is not a fact—unless he, himself,

makes it one by continuing to believe it. It is not a *fact,* because the fact is that he is past middle-age, so he is exactly the age when most large fortunes are amassed. The really great fortunes have been built by men much older than he, because it took them that long to learn fortune-making attitudes and techniques.

(2) "My family and I will live out our lives in disgrace and poverty." That, too, is only *his opinion.* It is not a fact—unless he, himself, makes it one by continuing to believe it. In the first place, losing money in unwise investments is no disgrace. Most investors make unwise purchases some time or other. Many investors have, at some time, lost most or all of their money. As previously pointed out, usually they get it all back and more, because fortune-making is a state of mind and a technique. So, instead of our friend's feeling "disgraced", he should feel that he has learned a lesson which will be of great value in his future decisions.

As for him and his family's living in poverty for the rest of their lives, that not only is an *opinion,* not a fact—but it is a ridiculous opinion, as previously pointed out. The only danger is that it is an *opinion* which he has mistaken for a fact—and, accepting *opinions,* yours or someone else's, as being *facts,* can ruin you!

Opinions are a dime a dozen—and not worth that. Facts are worth their weight in gold. Literally!

Build your life—decision by decision—soundly based on *facts* that you can accurately trace back to their very origins, so you can be sure that they really are exact, provable facts.

You can mistake an error for a fact and reach a very wrong decision, just by failing to trace your fact to its exact origin—as dramatized by the following story:

In the early days of the telephone, when one had to turn a crank to ring up the operator, a man furiously turned the crank every day just before noon. It seemed that he was desperate to reach the operator at just before noon every day to find out exactly what time it was. After some weeks of courteously telling him the time from her own watch, the operator finally asked who was phoning. He replied importantly, "I am the man who blows the whistle of the town factory exactly at noon."

"That's a coincidence," replied the telephone operator, "I've been telling you the time from my watch which I set by your noon whistle!"

How sure are you of *your facts*? The dependability of the judgments upon which you will stake your entire future depends upon your ability to separate *facts* from *opinions*—and to reach your decisions based on *facts*—facts which you can depend on because you have traced them to their origins.

Chapter 6

Then I Found The Gray Area

Time was, years ago, when I thought that everything was black or white. On one extreme or another, I would take my stand. And stand. Immovable.

I would be like General Grant and "hold the line if it took all summer." I would do even better. I would maintain my fixed position if it cost me every friend, if it cost me every cent!

I would be like Martin Luther and nail my convictions to the door. I would do even better. My convictions would be more than a statement of belief. They would be an open challenge to everyone!

I would be like the executive who put a sign on his desk facing his callers. The sign read: "Be reasonable. Do it *my* way."

I would not be a middle-of-the-roader. Hadn't I read, "Most accidents happen in the middle of the road"?

But I'm older now. And with the passing of years, I've changed—I might even say I've learned. Years of watching others succeed . . . so smoothly . . . so pleasantly . . . so surely . . . have taught me a better way to success. And a better way of life.

I've outgrown building a fortress around my demands. The immobility of a fortress makes it a prison.

Besides, who needs a fortress if he has no demands to defend? A fortress serves no purpose in moving forward toward a goal—and that is what Life really is all about.

Then I found the gray area. Everything really isn't black or white—right or wrong—at all. It only looks that way to youth and to those adults whose minds haven't grown up. Hence all those silly protest marches, and sit-ins, stand-ins, teach-ins—and, even worse, some very radical believe-ins. All dramatized, of course, by the exhibitionists.

But the world smiles understandingly at the adolescent behavior—not its misguided exploiters—then goes about its important business in the gray area which I didn't know about, either, when I was young and inexperienced.

Yes, the gray area, where the black and white edges of extremism blend into understanding and agreement.

The gray area where everybody's point of view can be respectfully considered, where everybody gives a little and gets a little, where negotiation may be hard or may be persuasive, but leads, if we just work at it enough, to the hand-clasp of mutual resolution.

The gray area, where, if we just keep talking long enough, we can agree on something worthwhile.

The gray area, where a President of the United States can say to all men, friend and foe alike, "Come, let us reason together. Then we can find a consensus."

I'm glad I've matured enough to know that everything in the world isn't black or white—but, in between these two extremes is a blending of ideas and opinions in a vast gray area where men of good-will can meet and talk over their differences until at last the differences blend into one goal.

I'm glad I found the gray area. I hope you have found it, too.

Chapter 7

Conquest of Fear

There are a number of emotions which can be so overwhelming that they swamp our beings, wreck our personalities and make our lives almost unbearable. And not just "almost" unbearable. Sometimes so terribly unbearable that they are the principal causes of suicide and murder!

Hate, revenge, jealousy, sense of guilt, withdrawal and, the subject of this chapter: FEAR. These emotions are so destructive of happiness and often of life—physically, mentally and emotionally—that we shall discuss some of them, and perhaps all, elsewhere in this book. But right now, we're going to engage in the conquest of fear.

If you could be free from fear—all fear of everything and everybody—your life would be much better, wouldn't it? Well, within the next few minutes you will have the means of eliminating all fear—forever!

First, you have to drag your fears out into the open so you can get at them. That may seem surprising to those of you whose fear is all too real—so real, so definite, that its terror haunts you day and night—and is surely, methodically tearing you to pieces! Relax, we'll soon get rid of it! Open fears are easily eliminated. It's the hidden fears, the disguised fears, which cause the most trouble. But only because they are hidden. So let's go on a fear-hunt.

Each of us has, as you know, a conscious mind which gives us our awareness of everything around us, does our conscious reasoning and is subject to our personal direction and will.

Also, as you know, each of us has a subconscious mind which functions at a much deeper level and which not only operates our bodily activities (our heart-beat, breathing and all the rest of our complicated bodily mechanisms), but also—because it is a part of the all-powerful Universal Mind which runs the whole universe—actually brings into reality our self-image (what we have led it to believe *we* really want to *be*).

Of course, the foregoing descriptions of our conscious and subconscious minds are greatly over-simplified. I just want to identify them because it is in our subconscious minds that we are going to conduct our fear-hunt.

If our fears were in our conscious minds—and some of them are—we would have no trouble recognizing them and, as described later, eliminating them. But when our fears have been implanted in our mysterious subconscious minds, they are either deeply hidden or strangely disguised. We therefore have to dig them out, rip away their disguises, and get them into our conscious minds where we can easily dispose of them.

Often you can find these hidden fears, yourself, now that you are aware that they are likely to be hidden or disguised in your subconscious mind. It is not the function of this book to get into the details, but merely to point out the necessity of a fear-hunt for hidden and disguised fears and to start you on your way.

Some of the symptoms of hidden and disguised fears are: (1) withdrawal from normal activities; (2) unexplained feelings of anxiety; (3) unexplained tension; (4) psychosomatic illness, an illness (real enough!) which has no physical cause, but usually is a form of withdrawal, and accounts for over half of the patients of all doctors and in all hospitals! The list could go on and on, but any of the foregoing or similar symptoms probably indicates you have a hidden or disguised fear lurking in the depths of your subconscious.

On your fear-hunt, ignore the symptoms which disguise your fear and try to trace the cause to the real fear, itself. Not being any longer deceived by disguise, you often can find it, drag it out into the open, rip off its disguise and treat it like any other fear—eliminating it forever by the methods we shall describe.

If you personally can't find your hidden or disguised fear, by all means get professional help from a psychologist or psychiatrist.

In any event, the important thing is to know what fear you are dealing with. Then eliminate it by one, several or all of the following methods:

(1) DELIBERATELY, UNHESITATINGLY, DO THE THING YOU FEAR! Impress on yourself that you ARE doing the thing you fear . . . voluntarily . . . deliberately . . . without hesitation! Not timidly—but boldly! You probably still will experience the feeling of fear at first. Good! Emphasize the feeling of fear! *Over*-emphasize it! Then deliberately . . . unhesitatingly . . . *do the thing you fear!* Laugh in its face! Ridicule it! Stare your fear down! Kick it around! Trample it! Keep aware that you ARE doing the thing you fear—and to hell with it! You are going to do it anyway!

(2) REPEATEDLY DO THE THING YOU FEAR! Over and over again! Literally wear your fear out. (If you want to be scientific about it, this is called the: "FEAR EXHAUSTION METHOD".) But by any name, the technique is to repeatedly *do the thing you fear* until you don't fear it any more! Not even the least bit!

(3) LAUGH AT YOUR FEAR! The one thing that fear can't stand is to be laughed at. Taunt it! Sneer at it! Mock it! Make fun of it! And all the time, *keep doing the thing you fear* . . . deliberately . . . unhesitatingly.

(4) BE A FATALIST! I'll always remember the gangster who was involved, as usual, in a gang war with a rival gang. One night, he and two companions were shot at from an ambush. A companion on each side of him was shot dead. Miraculously, he was unharmed. Later when reporters asked if he wasn't afraid that the other gang would "get" him, too, he just shrugged and said, "We've all gotta go sometime, somehow". He was willing

to take life—and death—as it came, and he wasn't about to have the least fear of either.

(5) DEPEND ON THE LAW OF AVERAGES! By the Law of Averages, most of the things we fear never happen. The chances are so overwhelmingly in your favor that it is ridiculous to live in fear! Nobody is absolutely safe anywhere, any time. But you are reasonably safe. And that is a lot better than being unreasonably afraid.

(6) GET ALL THE FACTS! Not opinions—facts! Most fears have as their base the primitive fear of the *unknown.* When you have learned all there is to know about whatever is causing your fear, you will find that your fear has vanished under the bright light of knowledge. Most people who are afraid, are afraid of learning the truth. They are afraid they will find out "for sure" that they have a serious disease, or that their husband is having an affair with another woman, or that they may lose their job. Then—right then—is the time to apply the method of *"know the thing you fear"*

Get the truth, the whole truth, that you are afraid of. An early diagnosis of a serious disease has saved many lives.

Find out if your husband's affair is fact or gossip; then if it is a fact, see a marriage counsellor or an attorney. Don't let suspicion and fear eat your heart out. Get busy doing something sensible and constructive about it. In any event, you'll eliminate your fear with the bright light of knowledge.

If you are afraid you are going to lose your job, find out the fact from the man who knows—your boss. Ask what you can do to keep it. You may have faults that can be corrected. And your boss will appreciate your forthright attitude. If losing your job is inevitable, the sooner you find out about it, the earlier head-start you will have in looking for a better job.

Remember these sure cures for fear: (a) getting all the *facts;* and (b) taking immediate, positive *action.*

(7) MAKE YOURSELF FEAR-PROOF! You can block fear out of your life by establishing in your mind and emotional system a positive, overwhelming response to any negative fear you may anticipate. In that way, you make yourself *fear-proof*. For example, I grew up in a neighborhood where, as a timid boy, I was constantly "picked on" by bigger, tougher boys. This implanted in my conscious and subconscious minds, as I grew up, the fear that others could bully me, "push me around" and, if I timidly resisted, "beat me up".

So I made myself fear-proof by learning boxing and, later, Judo, Super-Judo, Karate, Aikido, Savate, Yawara and deadly Kung Fu. That's just about as protected as any human can get. Even after retirement, I keep in condition by exercise every day using calisthenics, dynamic-tension, isometric-contraction and weight-lifting. This not only is good for my physical condition, but it is even better for my mental and emotional condition. I have, in the field of self-defense, made myself fearproof, which not only has given me physical confidence, but is rewarding mentally and emotionally.

The process of making yourself fear-proof in any field which may have the seeds of fear is very satisfying as well as being personally beneficial. Take swimming, for example. Suppose you are afraid of the water; afraid of drowning. You can spend so much time in the water that you will be perfectly "at home" there—without the least fear. Get a good swimming instructor. Learn to be an expert in all the strokes, especially swimming under water. Learn skin-diving. Learn "drown-proofing", which now is being taught by the Red Cross and some universities and which is a simple method of keeping safely afloat for hours unlimited. Soon you will be as much at ease in the water as you will be on dry land. You will have become fear-proof of water and you will have added a most pleasant experience to your enjoyment of life.

(8) HAVE A DEEP RELIGIOUS FAITH. It is not the purpose of this book to intrude into your personal religious beliefs or your lack of them. But any discussion of the conquest of fear would be incomplete without pointing out that more lives have been kept free of fear by deep, constant religious faith—than by any other method.

This concludes our Conquest of Fear. If you use one, several, or all of the methods given here for the elimination of your fear or fears, you will rid your life of one of its greatest burdens. You will gain a new sense of freedom and power. You will feel like—and you actually will be—a Conqueror! A Conqueror of Fear!

Chapter 8

Give Your OWN Wonder Drug

Do you know that you *now* can make your *own* wonder-drug in unlimited quantities? It is one of the most powerful wonder-drugs in the world! You can make it easily—provided that you give it away. The more you give away, the more you can make. It will cost you nothing and pay you enormous dividends!

Here are a few of the many miracle results you can get by giving this wonder-drug which you make yourself:

(1) School children, when given your wonder-drug, will study more eagerly and get much higher grades.
(2) Business associates, when given your wonder-drug, cooperate with you, help lift you to success and wealth.

(3) Your family and friends, when given your wonder-drug, will think you are wonderful and be eager to be with you.

(4) You, with your wonder-drug, will spread happiness wherever you go.

(5) When giving your wonder-drug, you will get enough of it on yourself to make you happy, successful, popular and rich.

Since there is a law against making exaggerated claims for drugs, we had better be quick with the proof of the foregoing claims for your wonder-drug.

First, we will have to identify it, give its exact name.

It is: PRAISE!

What? Such a simple thing as *praise*, a wonder-drug which will work miracles?

Yes! PRAISE is a wonder-drug and it will work miracles! Let's ask one of the foremost psychiatrists in the world, Dr. Alfred Adler. Dr. Adler told his patients who were the unhappy victims of anxieties, fears and depression, "You can be *cured* in 14 days if you think constantly how you can *please* someone."

And what is the best way to *please* someone? What is it that people want more than anything else in the world?

Let's call in another authority, another of the foremost in the world: the famed William James of Harvard, America's greatest philosopher-psychologist. William James said, "The deepest principle in human nature is the *craving to be appreciated.*"

The way to satisfy this "deepest principle in human nature" . . . this "*craving to be appreciated*" is by your *praise.*

Therefore, *praise* not only puts into effect the wise teaching of William James, but it fulfills Dr. Adler's prescription to *please* someone.

So among the miracle-cures of your wonder-drug, *praise,* you have it on the highest authority that it will *cure* anxiety, fear, depression in just 14 days!

Now let's prove the other claims we made for your wonder-drug, *praise,* at the beginning of this chapter.

(1) In a scientifically supervised test, school children were *praised for* their intelligence and ability, and, at the beginning of the test, they were assured that the test would be *easy* for *them.* They responded to *praise* by doing much better than average and getting very high grades.

Then the same school children were given another test, equally easy, but were *criticized* and *harassed* before the test and told it was too difficult for *them* and that they would do poorly. The result was that they did very poorly and got very low grades.

The *only* difference: PRAISE . . . and more evidence that *praise* is a wonder-drug which produces miracle results.

(2) Business associates, when given your wonder drug, *praise,* will gladly cooperate with you, help lift you to success and wealth. Why? Because when you give them what they want: *praise*—they will give you what you want: *cooperation.* When you *praise* a business associate, you give him self-confidence and a sense of security. Criticize him and you make him feel insecure. He mentally labels you as the "hatchet man" who may cost him a promotion—or even his job! That's why *praise* is so important in

all business relationships. It not only makes people like you, but it makes them respond by helping you because you have made it clear that you will help them.

(3) Frequently *praise* your family and friends. They will think you are wonderful and be eager to be with you. Why? I can't say it better than William James, "The deepest principle in human nature is the *craving to be appreciated.*" Fulfill that craving with sincere *praise* and everybody will be eager to be with you.

(4) You, with your wonder-drug—*praise*—will spread happiness wherever you go. That, by now, should be self-evident. If it isn't, just try *praise*—everywhere—for just one week!

(5) When giving your wonder-drug—*praise*—you will get enough of it on yourself to make you happy, successful, popular and rich. That is because, when you turn the spotlight on others, the reflected glow illuminates you more than if you had tried to hold the spotlight on yourself. And, finally, *praising* others will give you the *mental attitude* necessary for success in life. As psychologist Dr. Walter Scott, President of Northwestern University, said, "Success or failure is caused more by *mental attitudes* than by mental capacities."

PRAISE is a form of giving. It is not only "more blessed to give than to receive", as the Bible tells us—but it is *necessary to give—in order to receive,* as life has an insistent way of reminding us.

So give the most desired gift of all. Give the gift that satisfies the "*craving to be appreciated*".

Give your own wonder-drug: PRAISE!

Chapter 9

Are You Fed Up?

Some time ago, on the front page of my newspaper, there was an article headed: "14 'Fed-Up' Bus Drivers Take New Jobs, Pay Cut". This article should interest us for a number of reasons:

(1) The editors of one of the leading newspapers in America felt that this event contained so much "human interest" that they featured it on the front page. Psychologists would say that a great many people would "identify" with the bus drivers who were "fed-up" with their dealings with other people. Apparently a lot of people are "fed-up" with their present jobs and their relations with others.

(2) What were the facts? According to the newspaper article, fourteen bus drivers in one large city quit their jobs and voluntarily took jobs as bus-cleaners at a substantial reduction in pay and with complete loss of job seniority up to eighteen years!

Why did they do this? These fourteen bus drivers who eagerly sacrificed so much to get out from behind the steering wheel and get behind a broom, gave these reasons:

(a) "Passengers hardly ever have the right change. They are always pestering us for change."

(b) "There's no feeling of cooperation between the passengers and us."

(c) "In the winter, kids throw snowballs at our bus."

(d) And again . . . "that pesky job of making change."

That's why these fourteen bus drivers gave up their jobs and long seniority to take lower-paying jobs as bus cleaners!

Now let's not be critical of those poor, harassed men. Many people have found peace and happiness by admitting that they were incapable of dealing with the trivial (and to them, annoying) aspects of human nature and then withdrawing to the relative seclusion of more solitary jobs. After all, somebody has to do this more menial work, and who is better qualified than those who cannot get along with their fellow men?

I would venture this guess, however. Most of those men who chose to clean buses will not find happiness in that work, either. The irritating passengers will not be there, but the debris they left behind, will be. After scraping thousands and thousands of wads of used chewing gum from beneath the bus seats, the cumulative effect may well be just as annoying as was the cumulative effect of "making change" for the passengers.

(3) In any event, the problem results from two common causes:

(a) Mentally and emotionally building up a triviality into a "big thing", instead of maintaining a reasonable perspective; and

(b) Allowing minor irritations to accumulate until they become an unbearable burden, instead of taking them in stride as a routine part of the job, ignoring and forgetting each trivial annoyance immediately.

As Lincoln said, "A man is just about as happy as he makes up his mind to be." I remember another story about a bus driver. This bus driver was happy with his work. It gave him a wonderful opportunity to meet people—thousands of people—all of whom he greeted with a big, cheerful smile. "Making change" gave him a little extra time to say something pleasant to his passengers. When he wasn't chatting happily with his passengers, he softly sang or whistled a gay little song. And when, after many years of such joyous service, he finally retired—his regular passengers gave him a big going-away party. Some of his passengers actually cried. And he cried a little, too. Warm tears of joy—for the opportunity of having been a bus driver, so he could make so many friends!

Yes, your *attitude* toward conditions, situations and people makes *all* the difference! As Mr. Lincoln said, "A man is just about as happy as he makes up his mind to be."

Chapter 10

Keep A Firm Foundation

This nation will stand firm or fall, depending upon the strength of the base upon which it is built.

That base is law.

The wisdom and fairness of our laws, the impartiality and certainty of their enforcement, and the deterring effect of inescapable, severe punishment for their violation, will determine the future of our country.

There is a growing laxity in all these areas.

There seems to be a purposeful permissiveness in some of our laws and regulations, which indicates a deliberate effort to placate vocal pressure groups within our society. This is neither wise nor fair. When laws are passed, revised or reinterpreted to benefit certain groups with the result that other individuals or groups are adversely affected, the regulatory system of this nation is being used improperly. The danger is quite clear. Laws are not intended for expediency—but for justice.

There is considerable variation in the degree of certainty with which our laws and regulations are enforced. We excuse this because of the human, and therefore variable, interpretations of the severity of the infractions. Law enforcement has become a somewhat personal prerogative of the individual or organization entrusted with seeing that laws and regulations are obeyed—strictly, exactly, within their full meaning and intent.

The situation in the field of law enforcement has become so lax that private citizens and pressure groups arrogantly and publicly announce that they will obey only those laws and regulations which suit their personal purpose and that they deliberately will openly disobey any law which, in their own individual judgment, is not to their benefit or is deterring their aims. No nation which tolerates such open and hostile defiance of its laws by its own citizens can long survive. Even the threat of such defiance should incur such disciplinary action as to make the act itself avoided because of the assured severity of certain punishment.

No individual, because he is a leader or a vocal member of a dissident pressure group, deserves immunity from, or should be given probated or trivial punishment for, deliberately and defiantly breaking a law or regulation. We have developed a fear of making martyrs because it might enhance their publicity and propaganda value. This is a dishonorable fear which can be eliminated by making the punishment for self-provoked martyrdom sufficiently severe to make it undesirable. Otherwise, we shall continue to have our law enforcement officials under frequent provocation by those who would use accusations against them to incite agitation for their objectives.

All levels of law enforcement would greatly be improved if the entire citizenry were thoroughly convinced that the violation of any law or regulation would result in inescapable, impartial and severe punishment. When I say "severe punishment" I mean so severe that its risk would not be justified.

Too many people are willing to play Russian roulette with crime because they know all of the cylinders of severe punishment are not loaded. They are being constantly indoctrinated with the current trend to light sentences, suspended sentences, paroled sentences, and punishment being deferred interminably by legal maneuvering. Only when punishment is certain, swift and severe, can it serve as a maximum deterrent.

Certainly, every intelligent effort should be made to rehabilitate criminals and, being very sure we have done so, to return them to freedom. But it is much better to prevent their becoming criminals in the first place. The preventive, or at least, the deterrent, is certain, swift and severe punishment.

Of course, the ultimate ideal is a total moral abhorrence of and abstention from, all crime by all people. It is a far distant state, but one which deserves constant seeking. However, in the meantime, the problem of increasing and flagrant law violation is here now. It must be dealt with by using the means at hand.

The very survival of this free nation depends upon respect for, and enforcement of, law and order. If it is necessary to improve the wisdom and fairness of our laws, the impartiality and certainty of their enforcement, and the deterring effect of inescapable, severe punishment for their violation—let us get on with the task.

This nation stands on the base of law. Let us be sure that foundation is firm and secure.

Chapter 11

Lunatics Never Unite!

Years ago, before improvements were made in mental hospitals, a visitor was escorted through a mental hospital by the superintendent. He finally was taken to a balcony overlooking a ward where the most dangerous "lunatics" were kept. One hundred violently dangerous lunatics, watched over by only three guards!

The visitor was aghast. He turned to the superintendent and asked, "Aren't you afraid those dangerous lunatics will gang up on the guards?"

The superintendent calmly replied, "No, *lunatics never unite.*"

There is a lesson in that statement for all persons, groups and nations. Evidently many of us haven't been sufficiently impressed by the wisdom which has come ringing down through the years:

"In union there is strength!"

"United we stand; divided we fall!"

Perhaps, we will be more impressed by the dramatic implication in: *"Lunatics never unite."*

To the extent that we, as people, as groups, or as nations, achieve unity of thought, unity of feeling, unity of purpose—to that extent will our strengths be joined.

The secret of power is no secret. It simply is uniting——joining together with a singleness of thought, feeling and purpose. The more people who can unite, the more groups which can be joined together, the more nations which can collaborate—the greater will be their combined power.

How much weakness there is in disunity!

And, how much danger! Because the farther apart our positions, the more nearly they become opposites. When we reach opposite positions, we are placed in readiness for the most damaging collision course.

Lunatics!

Yes, lunatics! That's what our divisiveness is proving us to be. Because: LUNATICS NEVER UNITE!

Chapter 12

Frustration Causes Aggression

Frustration-caused aggression is the basic factor in many human tragedies from personal incompatabilities to major wars.

Since frustration is a primary ingredient in almost all (some scientists say *all*) aggression—overt or repressed—it would be useless as well as impractical to attempt to list all such situations here. However, it may indicate their variety and magnitude, to list a few of many problems resulting from frustration-caused aggression:

Infant misbehavior, school failures, juvenile delinquency, unhappy marriages, business difficulties, disagreeable personalities, minority-group social-racial unrest, individual and group protest activities, riots, revolutions and wars.

Since the frustration-aggression sequence is at the root (and usually *is* the root) of so many, varied and tragic problems, it demands our most serious consideration.

It is the principal purpose of this book to stimulate thought, and no attempt will be made here to solve a problem of this magnitude. It simply is hoped that this chapter may, in its limited way, indicate areas of solution and direct your thoughts into channels which should be stimulating and productive.

To simplify our approach, let's accept the conclusion of many leading scientists that: *aggression is always a consequence of frustration. (Frustration and Aggression:* Yale University Press, New Haven, Conn.) And let us be quick to point out that frustration-caused aggression is not always overt and recognizable as aggression, but often is repressed and festers in our subconscious to later appear in some disguised resentment, hatred, antagonistic feeling or misbehavior. We have been taught to suppress openly aggressive acts, but this does not mean that the aggression, itself, actually is eliminated. It merely is repressed into our subconscious and, unless eliminated, can do incalculable harm.

Let's have a closer look:

An infant is subjected to many frustrating experiences which are all the more acute because the child is too young to understand the reasons for the drastic changes required in its behavior. Complete changes in food, eating habits, personal cleanliness and toilet training are just a few of the frustrations which accumulate to provoke the period of "frequent and exaggerated stubbornness" between the ages of two and four years, and which usually reaches its peak at the age of two and a half.

And then, as the child grows up, there are the frustrations of home life, school, and becoming a part of the social system of its group. Each frustration creates aggression—overt or suppressed.

Physical measurements, muscular coordination and intelligence tests show that the average boy or girl at the age of fifteen has, by any accepted criterion, the capacities of an adult, lacking only the experience and training which are acquired by most of us through later years. Otherwise, boys and girls of fifteen are adultly equipped to cope with their environment and to take part fully in the society of adults.

But boys and girls of fifteen are not considered to be adults by their elders. They are not respected as adults. They are not treated as adults and usually determined efforts are made to impress upon them their inferior status. Their activities are limited, their independence is not tolerated and many of the restrictions of childhood remain in force.

There is no doubt that many of the usual restrictions and limitations placed upon these young adults are necessary—socially, economically and morally. The manner and form in which these limitations are imposed are worthy of most serious consideration because when you treat an adult as a child—no matter how necessary and well-intentioned your motives—you cause the most intense frustrations. And "*aggression is always the consequence of frustration.*"

Now let's move our spotlight of thought to the subject of unhappy marriages. The rapidly increasing divorce rate is an inadequately low indicator (quantitatively and qualitatively) of unhappy marriages for too many obvious reasons to discuss here. It is sufficient to state that any marriage counselor will unequivocally assure you that most unhappy marriages are the result of *frustration* with its accompanying aggression, overt, or repressed into the subconscious where it may reappear as resentment, scorn, jealousy, bitterness, nagging, temper outbursts, easily hurt feelings and general unpleasantness. So, frustration and its resulting aggression are the prime causes of unhappy marriages.

And frustration goes on to other areas of life, to cause incalculable damage. Business, by its very nature —its complexities, constant personal contact, competition, change, ambition, pressure—is a spawning ground of frustrations of every description and magnitude. Not only does business cause frustrations, but it stimulates aggression by requiring competition within companies in the constant building and rebuilding of each corporate power superstructure.

When you combine ambitious power struggles at the higher levels, personality conflicts at all levels, and labor-management problems ranging from hostile disputes to violent strikes—all within one company environment—you have the ingredients which produce frustration and aggression on a grand scale!

Add to the intracompany frustration, the competitive aggression of the market place—and the result is the well-named Corporate Jungle. No wonder business men have ulcers, nervous breakdowns and heart attacks!

There is no easy solution to ending or even greatly reducing the frustration which is so firmly built into business. It is a part of the very nature of business, itself, for business is almost totally a competitive, aggressive struggle to achieve superiority or often even to survive.

Nevertheless, the elimination of as much business frustration as possible is one of the first orders of our time. This must be done or the internal friction it is causing will grind our business machine to pieces. High rewards will go to those who can reduce the frustrations within a business or turn those frustrations into non-aggressive channels.

Already much is being done to give competition in the market place a "game image" to relieve some of the frustrations, tensions and pressures of what some sales executives call "survival combat".

But perhaps the most dramatic example that "*aggression is always a consequence of frustration*" is found in the open aggression of minority groups, such as some Negroes in the United States. Here is the perfect example of almost every kind of frustration being accumulated and compounded over many years, until the inevitably resulting aggression has crashed upon the American scene with the release of pent-up hostility, uncompromising demands, provocative demonstrations, threats of violence and numerous riots.

Such mass aggression gives birth to leadership which escalates the group frustrations. Some leaders do this with social responsibility and exhortations to non-violence. Other leaders take advantage of the emotional extremism of the type of followers they attract and incite violent aggressiveness for the sheer exhiliration of their own demonstration of personal power.

Undoubtedly, the initial frustrations were justified. Undoubtedly, the conditions which caused them should be rectified and will, to a great extent, be alleviated in time. However, the violence and hostility of such mass aggression and especially the uncompromising demands accompanied by threats that all these demands must be met in full "now," has caused extreme frustrations among those millions against whom the aggression is directed. These frustrations have created a counter-aggressiveness which will retard fully-accepted solutions to these problems for years, leaving scars of overt and suppressed hatred and ill-will like those of the Civil War. Token and surface solutions may be forced for political advantages and men of good will, working with patience and moderation, will some day alleviate the hostility of the aggression and thus dissipate the defiant counter-aggression which it engendered.

It is extremely important to note that all Negroes in the United States were not frustrated, or to the extent to which they were frustrated, they directed their aggression into channels of personal achievement. In either case, their lack of hostile aggression has made possible their acceptance, popularity, acclaim and accomplishments which have far exceeded those of many white people. For example, there are Negro entertainers, athletes, educators, business men, government leaders and many other Negroes of whom this country is very proud and whom it accepts and admires with a feeling that is entirely non-racial.

This acceptance and integration of Negroes as complete equals to whites in every respect is demonstrated in the United States Armed Services. As a direct result of having eliminated the cause, there is no Negro frustration as to their status or acceptance as equal members of the Armed Services—and there is no aggressive feeling toward white fellow-soldiers. (If any frustration exists, the aggression it causes is soon dispelled by the necessity of directing it toward the enemy.) In the Armed Services, the equal, integrated, accepted, unfrustrated Negro has distinguished himself with skill, courage and heroism which has won the admiration of his white comrades and the entire nation.

When you compare the unfrustrated, successful Negro in civilian life or the unfrustrated, heroic Negro in the Armed Services with the frustrated, socially-aggressive Negro demonstrating, protesting, rioting in the streets—you have a dramatic example of the frustration-aggression cycle at work. And you can clearly see that as frustration is eliminated, aggression is eliminated.

You can analyze this on a much larger scale as a cause of wars between nations.

Nations, because of strong nationalist feelings, ethnic incompatibilities, desires to be superior and just plain greed, tend to actions and pronouncements which often cause frustrations in other nations. These national frustrations cause aggressive feelings in direct proportion to the degree of frustration. Too often, instead of diminishing or eliminating the frustration and the aggressive feelings which it provokes, each nation escalates the frustration-aggression cycle. The more the frustration-aggression is escalated, the less it is repressed, and the more overt and openly hostile it becomes. Unless this escalation is stopped or controlled, the ultimate result is war.

And so, now we have examined frustration-caused aggression from its early appearance in infant behavior, through adolescence problems, unhappy marriages, business difficulties, group protests and international relations. The list could be endless, but the categories discussed are sufficient to develop three conclusions:

(1) Aggression always is a consequence of frustration, and . . .

(2) Since frustration-caused aggression usually is, at best, disagreeable, and, at worst, disastrous—it should be avoided or eliminated, unless . . .

(3) The existence of the specific frustration-aggression is preferable to the consequences of avoiding or eliminating it.

The first two conclusions should now be obvious. The third should be emphasized, lest this chapter be interpreted as suggesting that tranquility be preserved at any price.

Therefore, before we examine various methods of avoiding or eliminating some of the frustrations which cause overt or repressed aggression, let us acknowledge that there are frustrations which we should not try to alleviate by submissive permissiveness—because the consequences of such permissiveness would be far worse than the aggressions resulting from the frustrations, themselves.

A few brief examples will suffice:

(a) Your young, inexperienced, teen-age daughter insists on staying out on dates as late at night as she chooses. If you restrict her dating hours, you will frustrate her desires, which include her status in her group. The result of the frustration will be shown in her aggressive attitude toward you, and result in unpleasantness in the home. However, you prefer that to the social, moral and other dangers which might result from her late-dating. So you restrict her dating hours and accept the results of the frustration-aggression caused by your restriction.

(b) Racial minorities, whose frustrations are justified and should be relieved, often have had their frustrations dramatized and further provoked by power-seeking leaders. This has caused such rapidly escalating aggression that they demand that all their grievances be redressed "now"—without regard for the chaos, frustrations and counter-aggression their threats and urgent demands have on the community. Many communities have not been panicked nor stampeded, but have chosen to restrain the frustration-aggression of the incited minority groups, while patiently and intelligently working to solve their problems with moderation and temperance—through cooperation.

(c) In international relations, certain countries, greedy for more territory and power, have claimed territory belonging to other countries. They incite frustation and aggressiveness among their own people and use this as a basis of threats. Nations capable of defending their presently established boundaries would be foolish indeed to succumb to such pressures of self-incited frustration-aggression on the part of their neighbors. It would not only be irrational, but suicidal, to retreat at every threat of an aggressive neighboring country.

It is apparent that I am not an advocate of the psychology of submissive permissiveness in any category from child-rearing to international relations. I believe that discipline (especially self-discipline, but imposed discipline, if necessary) will ultimately form stronger character than permissiveness.

I have little patience or respect for those who use the frustration-aggression sequence as a threat. That includes the child, teen-ager or adult who says (or demonstrates): "Unless you permit me freely to do whatever I want to do, I shall be frustrated and, as a result, I shall be aggressive in my feelings and reactions."

We hear that same type of threat from some leaders of racial minority groups, who say in effect: "We have a long and frustrating list of wants and unless we are given *everything* we want NOW, our frustration shall become aggression (in varying forms of violence, depending upon the extremism of the leader and his followers) and we shall be impelled to cause chaos, riot and revolt in the community." Now that kind of threat, and especially the immediacy of the demanded benefits, may panic some politicians into frenzied token compliance, but it inevitably creates a grass-roots counter-frustration-aggression which eventually retards the deserved improvements which could be gained by a more moderate, logical approach.

On an international level, nations use the frustration-aggression threat against other countries. Communist China currently is providing the most alarming example. Certainly, no other great country is so beset with frustrations. That most of China's frustrations are self-created does not make them less productive of aggressions which are violently hostile, internally as well as externally.

Of course, frustration is not the only cause of aggression, but it usually is present, sometimes as a cause, and often as a convenient excuse.

So, while the avoidance or elimination of frustration may not always be the best solution, it can, in so many instances, be of such great value that we should now see what can be done about it.

Basically, the avoidance or elimination of frustration and frustration-caused aggression can be accomplished by the following common-sense methods:

(1) Don't cause frustration in the first place. Discipline yourself to avoid imposing *unnecessary* restraints and inflicting *personal* irritations:

(a) Don't restrain, restrict or confine any person or group more than absolutely necessary.

(b) Don't impede another's progress toward his reasonable objective.

(c) Don't contradict or argue. Silence is usually more effective, anyway.

(d) Don't annoy. Being annoying is merely giving vent to your own frustrations.

(e) Don't obviously impose your will. Manipulate the situation so that the other person will think what you want is his own idea.

(f) Don't belittle, don't ridicule, don't detract

from the other person's feeling of importance, his desire to be admired, his favorable self-image.

(2) If frustration already exists—eliminate it. Then there will be no further cause for aggression.

(a) Stop doing the things which have caused the frustration. Subject every action which might possibly cause frustration, to the following test: Is this action ABSOLUTELY NECESSARY or is it merely an expression of my own personal preference? You will find that most restrictions, restraints, contradictions, arguments and annoyances are not ABSOLUTELY NECESSARY and the frustration-aggression they cause could easily be avoided by eliminating them.

(b) Reason away the frustration by "selling" the need for or desirability of the restraint or other action which MUST be taken. Restrictions and other often frustration-producing actions need not be frustrating. It usually is the manner in which they are imposed that provokes the initial feelings of frustration. Properly explained, *necessary* restrictions are accepted as being necessary, and therefore do not cause frustration. It is the parent who proclaims, "You may not do this . . . you may not do that!" . . . without explanation, and too often without a logical reason possible of explanation, who causes frustration-aggression in children.

(c) Immediately follow a frustration-creating action with a *substitute* offer which, if possible, is equal to, or more desirable than, the *necessary* restriction. For example, management says to labor, "We cannot pay all of the wage increase you ask, but we can modify your pension plan to provide even more money when you will most need it." Or, the parent says to the teen-age daughter, "You cannot have a date tonight because you need to study for your math exam, but you can have a birthday party at the club Saturday night."

(d) Take an *opposite* position to that which caused the frustration. For example: If you have caused a feeling of frustration-aggression by belittling a person and thus reducing his feeling of importance and damaging his precious self-image, take an opposite position; openly express your admiration for his good qualities, repairing the damage to his self-image by commendation and praise. Tactfully and sincerely done, this will erase the frustration.

(e) Eliminate or reduce the *feeling* of frustration. Remember, it is not what happens to a person, but how he *feels* about what happens, that really counts. Thus, if you can induce the *feeling* that the restrictions, restraints or whatever, are not of great consequence—if you de-emphasize their impact by not "making a major production" out of them—you, to that extent, directly de-emphasize the feeling of frustration.

(3) In some cases, you must eliminate, divert or suppress aggression first—before eliminating the frustration which caused it. (Always, you eventually must eliminate the frustration, too.) Here are some ways by which you can eliminate aggression:

(a) Psychiatrists call it "catharsis". This means that you drag the feeling of aggression out of the subconscious, expose it in the open, give it full expression and it will use itself up until it no longer exists.

(b) Don't let aggressive feelings get started. Use the same preventive methods just recommended for preventing frustration.

(c) Suppress the aggression until you can eliminate the frustration which caused it. Overt aggression can be suppressed in direct proportion to the severity of inescapable punishment. However, suppressed aggression leads to more frustration, which leads to more aggression. So don't suppress the aggression long—and work rapidly to eliminate the frustration which caused it.

(d) Channel aggression into beneficial activities, useful purposes. Aggression is not, in itself, evil or undesirable. Aggression can stimulate terrific energy which, if directed into worthwhile channels, can lead to great achievement. Many a mediocre person has become so aggressive against the frustrations of life which were holding him back, that he attacked his problems with such energy and determination that success was inevitable and his life goal was quickly attained.

I have tried, in this chapter, to outline some of the facts about the frustration-aggression cycle which is such a powerful factor at all levels, from infant behavior to international relations. In so limited space, it was not my purpose to fully solve many of the problems outlined, but I hope I have kept the promise in the title of this book and given you some "Thoughts To Build On".

Chapter 13

In All Fairness...

In all fairness . . . everyone should be alerted to an innocent-sounding word which can be used to rub a raw emotional nerve—with devastating effect.

Some time ago, I watched and listened to a political debate on television. This debate was followed by an hour radio program, during which the public was invited to telephone its comments on the debate. The telephone comments were broadcast directly so that all listeners could hear not only the spoken words, but the revealing tones of voice.

Anything I may have learned about the political issues debated was completely overshadowed by the revelation of an important aspect of human nature as disclosed by those telephone calls. Since you will be dealing with this same human nature all of your life, the following observations may serve as a reminder of a valuable lesson I'm sure you already know but which warrants reviewing.

Admittedly, I did not discover a new technique in dealing with people. This technique is one of the oldest, best-known and most effective. It is because of the last point that I feel it should be re-emphasized.

The debate itself was less than outstanding. It was characterized by an experienced politician-lawyer using an aggressive court-room manner to try to undermine the voters' confidence in the long voting record of his opponent, a distinguished senator who had served in public office for many years. The senator countered with a calm, sincere account of his seriously-considered reasons for voting as he did on the issues under debate.

Now, here is the important point: The senator also frequently emphasized that his opponent's accusations were "UNFAIR" because he said they were untrue, inaccurate or taken out of context.

It is not the purpose of this chapter to analyze the merits or the accuracy of either side of the debate. It is my purpose to point out the results of the use of the word: "unfair" which was so often used by the senator to characterize the accusations and statements of his opponent.

As previously mentioned, this debate was immediately followed by an hour radio program, during which listeners gave their opinions of it by telephone calls broadcast directly over the radio. With few exceptions, the opponent of the senator was vehemently attacked. He was called most of the derogatory names permitted on the radio. Long distance telephone calls were made to denounce him. And—note this—in almost every call, his performance in the debate was labeled: *"unfair."* All kinds of reasons were given for criticizing him, but they almost always also stated or implied that he was *"unfair."* The word or idea: *"unfair"* was the axis around which the criticism revolved.

Frankly, the vehemence of the first few radio-telephone calls rather surprised me. I had listened carefully to the debate, which was conducted with courtesy and decorum. Although they belonged to different political parties, there actually was little difference in the real political philosophies of either candidate. But, later, as the telephone criticisms continued to be broadcast, and as more and more members of even his party expressed their outrage at the *"unfairness"* of the one candidate's conduct of the debate, I sat back to absorb a refresher course in the emotional power of the word: *"unfair"*.

Few words in our language are so packed with emotional power. The accusation: "illegal" gives rise to judicial weighing of legal concepts and possible legal consequences. The accusation "untrue" also causes thoughtful, though sometimes resentful, consideration of the facts. But the word: *"unfair"* rubs a raw, emotional nerve. It builds sympathy for anyone supposedly treated *"unfairly"* and, at the same time, provokes often unwarranted hostility toward whoever is alleged to indulge in such unjust treatment of another.

People will accept with some tolerance many impositions which would seem to be more offensive, but when *"unfairness"* is accused, rational judgment is abandoned and hostile emotion takes over. Instantly there is the mental picture of the bully taking unjust advantage of the innocent underdog.

This was learned by labor unions in the early days of their organization. In fact, the word: *"unfair"* was so prevalent on picket signs, that its use by labor unions is included in the definition of *"unfair"* in the dictionary as an example of its use.

The fact is that the word: *"unfair"* is a push-button emotional word which can be used to attract sympathy to yourself and arouse hostility toward your opponent.

I am simply pointing out a powerful psychological fact. If you choose to use it, and how and to what extent you choose to engage in psychological warfare—is up to you.

Chapter 14

Plant Quarters – Reap Happiness

Did you ever find money?

When you were walking along a sidewalk or through a parking lot or in the aisle of a store, have you ever glanced down and found a bright, shiny quarter?

If you have unexpectedly found a quarter, think back and try to recall exactly how pleasantly surprised and happy you felt. You picked it up, perhaps looked at it for a moment with a feeling of being lucky, and maybe even told others of your good luck. Many people keep the money that they find. They put it in a special place as tokens of their good luck and as reminders that they are lucky.

Now, actualy there isn't anything very important about unexpectedly finding a quarter.

Or is there?

It isn't the value of the money. A quarter won't buy much these days. The value is in feeling that—suddenly—you are lucky! It may even start you feeling that now your luck has changed for the better.

Is this really important? Yes! Very important! Psychologists will tell you that it is not what happens, but how you *feel* about what happens, which actually matters. Mental capacities are not nearly so beneficial as mental *attitudes*. You become what you think you are.

And, it just so happens, that one of the most beneficial mental attitudes you can have is that *you are lucky*.

Success counselors will advise you to get and keep *"that lucky feeling."* Why? Because it makes you *expect* to get the good things in life. And what you *expect* to get—you *get!*

I want to encourage that *lucky attitude* in people. So I plant quarters for them to find. I stoop on the sidewalk to tie my shoe lace and place a quarter next to my shoe before I walk off. In a parking lot, I examine my rear tire and inconspicuously place a quarter beside it before driving away. In a store, I stop to examine merchandise and secretly leave a quarter beside it.

Of course, I never look back. I never stand around and watch to see who finds my quarters. That would spoil my imaginings of the delight of a lucky child, the surprise and unexpected pleasure of a grown-up who for a fleeting moment can become a child again, finding "treasure". If I don't look back, I can imagine what I will.

Like all coins, there are two sides to my planted quarters: the "good luck" feeling they give the finders and the fun I get playing this simple little game with Life.

Why don't you try planting quarters, too?

Chapter 15

Practice (In Your Imagination) Makes Perfect

The only way you can really become an expert in almost any endeavor is to practice intensively in your *imagination*. That's what the professionals do. And a professional either does it right—or he doesn't get paid. That's what the experts do—and that's how they got to be experts.

So practicing in your *imagination* is not some kind of hocus-pocus. It is the proper (and now accepted) use of the soundest psychological and physiological principles.

In golf you couldn't possibly think of all the things you must do to make a perfect drive, stroke or putt —*while* you are doing them—any more than you could consciously direct each intricate movement of your hands and fingers while playing the piano or typing a letter.

You simply cannot think that rapidly with your conscious mind, so that job is delegated by nature to your subconscious mind which operates at miraculous speed and with perfect accuracy. In fact, your subconscious mind directs almost everything you think, feel or do—from operating your heartbeat to providing the goal-seeking procedure by which you make a fortune if that's what you instruct it to do.

Let's see how you practice in your *imagination* (by using your subconscious mind) in sports. Take bowling. First, you must learn how to bowl with as perfect form as possible. You do this by taking lessons from an expert, by watching champions bowl and by studying the many excellent self-instruction books written and illustrated by the best bowlers in the world.

Then, having thoroughly learned exactly what to do, you practice. You practice in two ways: (1) Actual practice by really bowling (preferably under the watchful eyes of an expert instructor). (2) You practice each movement in your *imagination*, over and over again—having first learned to do it perfectly. It is absolutely essential that you know how to do it *perfectly*, before you practice in your *imagination*, because that's *exactly* how you will do it in the future.

How do you practice in your *imagination*? First, you relax in an easy chair in a quiet room away from all distractions. (You don't have to, but it's best.) Then you, mentally, take each *perfect* movement at a time and consciously visualize your performing that movement to perfection. Over and over again.

Actually you are impressing *mental pictures* of your executing the movement perfectly—into your subconscious mind. It is vital that you know that your subconscious mind cannot understand instructions from your conscious mind except in the form of *mental pictures.* If your subconscious is shown the word "lift", it will receive only the individual letters "L-I-F-T" which will mean nothing to it except how to spell the word. But if your conscious mind frequently impresses into your subconscious mind the *mental picture* of your imparting a "lift" to your bowling ball by squeezing your fingers at the instant of release, your subconscious mind will make that "lift" a part of your actual bowling delivery and you will get many more consecutive strikes because of the extra "spin" imparted to your ball.

It is a proven psychological principle that whatever *mental pictures* you impress into your subconscious mind, those exact *mental pictures* will be materialized into reality. So be sure your *mental pictures* are perfect.

That is the advantage of practicing in your *imagination.* You can practice *perfection.* But when you actually practice by physically performing all the intricate actions, you cannot concentrate on each rapid, individual movement to perfection and so you actually are practicing how to do it wrong instead of right.

Practice does not "make perfect," as the old saying used to tell us. Only practice of *perfection* makes perfect. And until you become a real expert, you can only practice *perfection* in your *imagination.*

Physical repetition of an action does not necessarily improve it. Certainly it does not assure perfection. You may only be teaching yourself how to do it wrong.

Remember the story about the new employee at the sawmill. The foreman had just instructed him in the use of a large, powerful electric saw. As the foreman turned away, he heard the new employee yell, "Ouch!"

When the foreman rushed back to see what had happened, the new employee explained, "All I did was just put my hand over here . . . well, I'll be damned—there goes another one!"

Mere physical repetition does not assure perfection—or even improvement. You must first learn the proper form. Then practice *perfection* in your *imagination* by consciously impressing into your subconscious mind *mental pictures* of your performing each action perfectly. Only then are you ready to physically practice and get the physical "feel" of what you have mentally practiced.

That's how the pros do it, that's how the experts do it—in every sport and, in fact, in all situations which require practice to develop proficiency such as public speaking, selling, meeting people, and just about every situation you can imagine.

One of the most distinguished, poised and charming women of our time says that she never enters a room full of people without first stopping to practice in her *imagination* how she will greet each person with friendly confidence, poise and charm.

If practicing in *imagination* is the proven way to perfection—why don't YOU do it, too?

Chapter 16

How To Survive

We hear a lot about survival, these days. Survival from this danger. Survival from that danger. It all sounds so ominous.

Perhaps we had better make our own do-it-yourself survival kit.

Let's start by looking at history and see how survival has been accomplished—starting all the way back to the beginning of life on this planet.

Basically there have been two consecutive steps to survival throughout the ages:

(1) FIRST . . . ADJUST to your existing environment.

(2) Having *first* adjusted, CONSTANTLY IMPROVE what you then are.

Let's see how these two survival steps worked in the past and how they will work in the present.

First, the principle of adjusting to existing environment: In prehistoric ages and throughout the long evolution of plant and animal life, only those plants and animals which adjusted to their changing environment survived.

Those plants which did not adjust to the changing temperatures, soil, moisture and other growth factors simply did not survive. Those which did adjust, took the first necessary step in survival.

The early forms of animal life had to do the same thing—and more. Animal life had to adjust to the elements—and it also had to adjust to living in the same environment with other animals. This adjusting to living in the same environment with other animals consisted of fleeing safely when attacked or defeating the other animals in combat, or "joining them" by making some accommodation which would permit living peacefully together.

Now, let's examine the second necessary step to survival, which is: Having first *adjusted* to your environment, you must *constantly improve* what you then are. This is the "law of the jungle". It also is a fundamental law of life. Survival depends, not only on adjustment, but on constant improvement which will enable you to keep up with or, preferably, to surpass competition within your environment.

For example, in plant life, a pretty little flower might be well adjusted to the elements of its environment, but not improve in such a way as to prevent being smothered out of existence by other plants which constantly improved in growth, size, strength and in rapidly expanding their area coverage.

An animal might adjust to its natural environment and its relations with other animals and thus temporarily survive—but if that animal did not improve at a rate equal to, or exceeding, that of competing animals, it soon would become so inferior that it would no longer survive the competition of the other animals which had become increasingly superior.

Thus, by a study of the history of evolution of all plants and animals, we find that the two steps for survival set forth at the beginning of this chapter have been necessary from the first stages of life on this planet to and including the present.

So let's see how these two steps for survival apply to various situations in present times and let's start with a specific example: YOU!

Let's apply step number one: Adjust to your existing environment. In your family, home, neighborhood, job, business; wherever you are at any time—you *first* must "fit in," adjust, cooperate, participate and (you may not like this word) conform.

What? In a free country? Can't you do what you like?

Can't you be unconventional? Can't you express your individuality, no matter how radical? Why must you "fit in," adjust, conform?

The answer is quick and simple: You must *first* "fit in", adjust, conform, in order to "survive". Of course, I don't mean "survive" in terms of life and death, although that sometimes has been the case. I mean "survive" in terms of being an effective, acceptable, compatible personality.

And especially note the word: "*first.*" You must *first* "fit in", adjust, cooperate, participate and conform in your relations to your family, home, neighborhood, job, business environment. You *first* must make whatever adjustments are necessary to make you acceptable. That gets you "in" on the best possible terms. Do otherwise and you just won't be accepted; you'll arouse opposition, antagonism—and reap a harvest of trouble.

Then, having *first* made whatever adjustments are necessary to conform to the established requirements of your environment and thus having been accepted as a welcome part of the group—you can put the second principle of "survival" into effect and begin the process of improvement.

Let's look at these two principles of "survival" in a specific instance. Let's assume that you have been promoted to a position of executive responsibility in your business. If you start out by not adjusting to your new environment, if you do not conform to the expectations of those who promoted you, if you do not cooperate, participate, "fit in", make yourself an acceptable part of the management team—you will not "survive" in your new job. Not doing what is required to be "in", you soon will be "out"—because you violated the first principle of survival: *first . . . adjust* to your environment.

Now, let's suppose you use this first principle of survival. You adjust to all of the requirements of your new job environment; you do everything to conform fully to the expectations of those who promoted you; you cooperate wholeheartedly with all company policies; you participate enthusiastically in all company activities; you "fit in" perfectly as an accepted, welcome member of the management team. Naturally, you "survive" in your new job. Why? Specifically, because you have used the first principle of survival which has been proven throughout the ages since the very beginning of life, itself.

So, being "in", accepted, safe, secure—you are in a position to use the second principle of survival: Having *first* adjusted—*improve* what you then are. So begin improving yourself, your work-effectiveness, your employee-management cooperation. Take, as your business motto: "How can I do it better?" Make constant improvement a way of life.

The unaccepted outsider who demands improvement of our business, social, or political structure will generate great annoyance, irritation, resentment and resistance—while the accepted conformist can work from the inside for gradual, acceptable improvement at a rate adjusted to the tolerance of that which is to be improved.

The teaching of *first* adapting, adjusting, "fitting in," conforming, will not be welcome or acceptable to the exhibitionists, egocentrics, show-offs and all those who are burdened by a warped psychosis which can only be fulfilled by attracting attention to themselves by their own non-conformity.

Nor will the lessons of this chapter be accepted by the revolutionaries who attempt to force, emotionally or physically, their own selfish "improvements" on society from outside the established social structure.

As this is being written, the vast nation of China, which once was the seat of world culture, learning, progress and power, has become a depressing example of the results of being unwilling to adapt, adjust and conform in any way to any of the various forms of political, social, economic and moral concepts held by progressive nations throughout the world. Instead, China persists in vainly attempting to impose its own archaic political, economic and social philosophy on underdeveloped nations by infiltrated revolutionaries from within and open aggression from without.

As a result, China is ostracized by the outside world and shattered within its own borders. The corrections which China needs to make are clearly evident from the lessons of this chapter.

Coming closer to home, we have what amounts to a kind of Negro revolution here in the United States. The problem, its cause and cure are far too vast and complex to analyze here. I simply want to apply the two-part formula, discussed in this chapter, to what is probably the most difficult and sensitive part of the Negro problem—the integration of Negro families into all-white neighborhoods. There is more white resistance to this than any other form of integration. Why?

Surveys have been made in all-white neighborhoods to find out what are the real reasons for the white families' rejection of Negro families as neighbors. Know what the real reasons are? You have just read about them in this chapter!

White families are afraid that Negro families will not ADJUST, ADAPT and CONFORM to the white families' standards of morality, cleanliness and maintenance of property values. The white families interviewed emphasized time and again that it was not the color of the Negroes' skin to which they objected, but they said that they would be afraid to go out on the street at night . . . they were afraid that the Negroes would not "keep up" their property and cause the neighborhood to become "run down." They felt sure, almost without exception, that property values would decrease. I won't continue the list of anticipated fears and grievances—but I assure you that every one reflected the white families' firm belief that the Negro families moving into their neighborhood would (1) NOT ADJUST, NOT ADAPT and NOT CONFORM to the present all-white neighborhood standards; they felt that the Negro families would not "fit in" and (2) that the Negro families would NOT IMPROVE the neighborhood, once they moved in.

That is the real problem and until white families feel *sure* that those conditions will *not* take place—all the civil rights laws, Negro demonstrations, protest marches and riots will only aggravate the problem, not solve it.

Until men and women of good will—Negro and white—work together to solve *that* problem with the proven principles set forth in this chapter, little progress will be made. Being a good neighbor, maintaining and improving the neighborhood, obviously has no connection with the color of one's skin.

The neighborhoods in which most Negroes unfortunately have been compelled to live have created an unfavorable image, which is not justified. This unfavorable image cannot be improved by Negro activities which arouse white antagonism and hostility. On the contrary, what is needed is a persistent effort to obtain justice with good will, and to provide Negroes with living conditions which offer them an equal opportunity to conform to the highest neighborhood expectations of white communities. Wherever this has been done, the Negroes have demonstrated their ability to achieve acceptance, not by demanding it, but by *deserving* it—which is the only way acceptance can be achieved. The emphasis must be placed—not on mere permission, obtained by legal or other means—but on deserved acceptance as a good neighbor.

The principles which originated with the beginning of life on this earth and which are just as valid today, surely are worthy of your most thoughtful consideration. Have you tried applying them to the various phases of your *own* life?

Do you ADAPT, ADJUST, CONFORM to the highest expectations of all the other people in your life? Having done this, do you then CONSTANTLY IMPROVE?

Do you?

Chapter 17

"This, Too, Shall Pass"

Long ago, William Cowper wrote: "The darkest day, lived till tomorrow, will have passed away."

It has always been, and always will be, so.

Each of our lives will have dark days. And each dark day will pass. Life, in the wake of its insistent imposition of tragedy, recants to soothe the hurt with gentle kindness—another day. And we should let it.

Let our dark days pass and be submerged in the acceptance which heals our wounds with gradual forgetfulness. Do not renew the darkness again and again on successive tomorrows but "let the dead past bury its dead".

Nothing worldly lasts forever. Most troubles, unless renewed, last but for a little while. You can face worry, grief, fear and hardship knowing that: "these, too, shall pass away". So when confronted with the inevitable, be willing to have it so. There is nothing you can do about it anyway. So do not cling to it overlong. Avoid the futility of scrubbing the deck of a sinking ship; if it must sink, it will. You need, instead, to seek another passage.

The door to the future awaits you. Do not linger behind, looking at a door from the past which has just closed. It is a law of life that when one door closes, another opens. We spend too much time looking with regret at the closed door when we should seek the open door and move on.

There is much inner strength in knowing that the darkest day will surely pass. And there is strength, too, in knowing that you never are given a burden which you are unable to bear. It is only when you cling to old burdens, so that you still carry the weight of yesterdays when you add the burdens of each new day, that you falter and break.

Sufficient unto each day are the burdens thereof. And sufficient is your strength for each day's burdens. As Dorothy Dix wrote: "I stood yesterday; I can stand today; I will not permit myself to think about what might happen tomorrow."

But what about tomorrow, when today's dark hours have passed? Of only one thing you can be sure. Tomorrow will be different—because the only certainty in life is change. You cannot control what changes tomorrow will make, but you can influence these changes in your life —for better or for worse—by your attitude toward each event and what you do about it. You have a choice, in attitude and action, so that when life gently closes its door on a dark day, you can seek and find a door, newly opened, through which you can walk . . . courageously . . . expectantly . . . into a brighter tomorrow.

Chapter 18

Forget It!

So some little incident, some little annoying harrassment, irritates you? Forget it! Forget it *now!* At once! Give it no further thought.

It will be obliterated by the profusion of events which will, in turn, occupy your attention next week, next month, next year. So you will forget it anyway, sooner or later. Why not *now?* Why make yourself unhappy for even one precious minute of your life by harboring resentment, anger, irritation, annoyance at some minor incident which you are going to forget sometime, anyway?

Your mind, as a kind of self-defense, will evade unpleasant, irritating thoughts and tend to turn to more pleasant areas of interest. So, sooner or later (and probably sooner) you are going to forget the minor annoyances of today. So why let them interfere with your happiness now? Why let yourself get emotionally stirred up by some insignificant happening which you won't even remember a week from now, a month from now or a year from now?

How quick and complete a forgetter you are, will have a considerable effect on your own personal happiness and the happiness of others involved, as you go through life. So here are a few helpful suggestions:

(1) Whenever you are the victim of some petty annoyance or irritation, ignore it and forget it *at once.* You are going to forget it anyway, sooner or later. Forget it *now!* Don't let some thing you are going to forget at some later time give you a week's, a day's, or even an hour's unhappiness. Forget it *now!* How? Here's how:

(2) Your mind instinctively wants to spare you unpleasantness—so help it by . . .

(3) Ignoring the annoyance and occupying your thoughts and activities with other projects as far different and as far removed from the annoyance as possible.

(4) Don't escalate the irritation, don't rub salt in a raw emotional wound, don't argue, don't respond irritably—in fact, just don't respond at all. Let the source of annoyance draw an emotional blank.

Life's little irritations and annoyances can add up to a large amount of unhappiness—yes, and high blood pressure, ulcers and all sorts of emotional disturbances—if you hold on to them until they pile up into a sizable burden.

So, get rid of them as they come—by being too thick-skinned to be bothered by little emotional mosquito bites, by ignoring or forgetting at once all minor annoyances as they come.

Don't wait for time and a cooperative or poor memory to heal your little wound. Don't suffer at all! Forget it NOW!

Chapter 19

Push Your Wheelbarrow Upside Down

A visitor to a mental hospital saw an inmate pushing a wheelbarrow upside down. When he asked the inmate why, the inmate replied, "You don't think I'm crazy, do you? I pushed this wheelbarrow right side up yesterday and they kept filling it with gravel."

On the basis of his reply, I think the inmate should be released and a lot of us put in his place.

Too many people, with the best of intentions, go around pushing their wheelbarrows right side up and permit almost anybody and everybody to dump their unwanted odd jobs, problems, worries and grievances into them. So they end up pushing the burdens of everybody else's gravel.

As you push your wheelbarrow through life, you'll find many people who will gladly put their burdens in your wheelbarrow. I suggest you push your wheelbarrow upside down. Be like the man who wrote God a letter and resigned as Manager of the Universe. Or as janitor!

He really didn't have to resign because he never was appointed. Nor was I! Nor were you!

He took the vast problems of humanity and heaped them in his wheelbarrow. Then he pushed his burden around with him wherever he went. He was unqualified, incapable and in no position whatever to solve these vast problems. (Nor am I. Nor are you!)

And when other people saw that here was a man going around collecting problems, they added their problems to his load. And he added quite a few of his own. Eventually his burden grew too heavy to bear. Both he and his wheelbarrow were about to break down, when he finally showed at least as much sense as the patient in the mental institution—he turned his wheelbarrow upside down! And he got instant relief from the useless pressure and worry of burdens which were not even his!

This is not a plea for indifference to the problems of others if your personal involvement can help. This is a plea for *selectivity*. You cannot solve all the world's problems, so why worry about them? Nobody elected me President of the United States, yet too often I find that I have assumed the burdens of the Presidency. I worry about what the President should do about this and what about that. Why? Why should I assume the worries and burdens of a job I don't want, wouldn't have, and couldn't get? Yet I worry as much about what the President ought to do as he does. So I'm turning my wheelbarrow upside down.

I read the daily papers as though they were directives from on High. I am gravely concerned about dozens of situations, and diligently try to decide what should be done about them. Yet none of these situations affects me. Most of them are in remote parts of the world—where I never have been and never expect to go. But I am solving their problems, although nobody has ever, in my whole life, asked me what my solutions would be! So I'm turning my wheelbarrow upside down.

I have been asked to serve as chairman of various charity campaigns. I may have qualifications along that line, but I have a neighbor across the street who is a real expert in that field. He was a major executive of a large corporation and devoted his spare time and great talent to charity fund drives, which he conducted with sensational success. Then he retired to devote his full time to charity. So if I am asked to lead a charity campaign, I shall properly put the job in his wheelbarrow, which is suitably built for just such a load.

This is not indifference on my part—but *selectivity*. Mrs. Kopmeyer and I have established the M. R. Kopmeyer Foundation, into which a substantial part of our estate subsequently will be channelled. It is a perpetual trust fund, the income of which will be devoted to the care and cure of crippled children for generation after generation. This is what we have *selected* to put in *our* wheelbarrow.

The point is: to be *effective*, you must be *selective* in choosing the responsibilities you will accept. If you push your wheelbarrow through life right side up, people will throw their problems, worries, unwanted tasks and responsibilities into it until you find yourself overburdened to the breaking point. And if, in addition, you, yourself, add world, national and general problems which are not your specific responsibility to solve, you surely will break under the load.

So push your wheelbarrow upside down until *you select* what *you* want its contents to be. Then your load, no matter how heavy, will seem light and will be a joy instead of a burden.

And you will have found a better, a happier, way of life.

Chapter 20

Those Big Signs All Of Us Wear

Psychologists try, somewhat vainly, to teach us that ALL of us wear big, invisible signs across our chests, reading:

"I want to be IMPORTANT."

"I want to be ADMIRED."

"I want to be APPRECIATED."

These big, invisible signs which *all* of us wear cannot be seen by your eyesight, but can be clearly read and understood by your insight. These signs serve two valuable purposes:

(1) They are WARNING signs, and

(2) They are DIRECTION signs.

Let us first consider how imperative is their *warning:*

When a person warns you that he wants to be *important,* to be *admired,* to be *appreciated* (as *every* person clearly does), you disregard his warning at great cost because you insure the inevitability of losing his friendship and the probability of incurring his enmity. It is incredible that we would disregard this infallible warning and ever do, say or write *anything* which would, even by implication, depreciate any of the three vital desires (and needs) which are at the sensitive center of every other individual's personality.

Yet, we do this constantly—and we will never know the cumulative cost to our own interests, desires and objectives, of our usually thoughtless disregard of this warning. I can only assure you that your loss is so great as to be incalculable when you disregard the warning clearly stated on the big, invisible signs which everybody always wears across his chest, warning:

"I want to be IMPORTANT."

"I want to be ADMIRED."

"I want to be APPRECIATED."

Be sure to visualize those signs every time you come face to face with *every* person—or write or phone him. They are the *necessary* basis for your dealings with all people . . . at all times . . . in all matters . . . under all circumstances! They are the very essence of success, itself!

And so, in addition to being warning signs which warn you where not to trespass, they are direction signs which clearly point the way in all your relations with others.

The sure path to success is to give others what they want or help them get it.

Since a person wants to be IMPORTANT (and everyone does), tell him he is important, treat him as an important person and, in every possible way, become an asset to his importance and an assurance that his importance will not be diminished.

Since a person wants to be ADMIRED (and everyone does), tell him that you admire him, tell others that you admire him, and show your admiration for him as a person, for his achievements, his family, his possessions. Do all these things tactfully, even subtly—because nothing is more offensive than insincere flattery of another for your own direct or indirect gain. So be *sure* that your admiration is genuine and sincere. You can do this by diligently seeking those attributes and possessions you sincerely can admire. You'll be surprised (and, I hope, pleased) at all the admirable qualities, accomplishments, relations and possessions other people have—if you just make a sincere effort to look for them! And, you'll find the effort well worth while.

Since a person wants to be APPRECIATED (and everyone does), show your appreciation in every possible way. Unlike admiration, which might be suspect of insincerity if not tactfully done, there is hardly any way in which you are likely to overdo appreciation. In fact, appreciation is almost always too little and too late—and given with too little imagination!

To fully express appreciation in the usual ways will earn you a degree of distinction because appreciation is seldom fully expressed, if at all. But to use a little imagination, to go to a little extra trouble and expense in order to more deeply express your appreciation will mark you as a person for whom it is especially pleasant to do favors.

The methods by which you can imaginatively express appreciation are so varied and unlimited, I shall leave them to your own invention—and only suggest a few:

(a) Instead of just a "thank you" note, send a telegram. It's quick and easy to dictate a telegraphic "night letter" over the phone to a Western Union operator. And "night letter" telegrams are very inexpensive. But such a "thank you" telegram will surprise, please and impress the recipient. (Be sure it is marked: "Deliver—do not phone," because a delivered telegram is more impressive.)

(b) If you have informally expressed your appreciation by phone, then promptly confirm it by registered mail, starting your letter with tongue-in-cheek formality such as: "Confirming my telephone conversation of this morning, I want to make it a matter of written record; therefore I say . . . 'Gee, *thanks!!!*'"

(c) Just the right little "thank-you" gift with an accompanying note is evidence that you are thoughtful as well as grateful—*if* the gift is appropriate, unusual and *inexpensive*. An expensive gift gives the impression that you are trying to "pay off" the obligation, instead of sincerely expressing appreciation for a favor.

Those are just a few ideas I know will work. You can take it from there.

More important: remember that ALL of the people you deal with have big, invisible signs across their chests, which warn and direct:

"I want to be IMPORTANT."

"I want to be ADMIRED."

"I want to be APPRECIATED."

Heed the warnings and follow the directions of those signs—and you will be amazed at the immediacy and extent of your personal success!

Chapter 21

Count Your Blessings

Schopenhauer, the philosopher of gloom and doom, did give us the basis for at least one happiness-producing technique when he said, "We seldom think of what we have, but always of what we lack."

Thank you, sir; we'll take it from there!

The easiest way to be unhappy is to spend a lifetime . . . or a day . . . or an hour . . . or even a minute . . . regretting what we do not have.

This is the quickest way to be unhappy, because it is always available and the material is abundant. Each of us, no matter how fortunate, can think of an unlimited number of things we would like to have, but have not.

So, if we choose, we can spend a lifetime suffering the bitterness of regret. Or a lesser time—since the choice is ours.

But who wants to? Do *you*? If so, rush to your nearest psychiatrist! Or thoughtfuly read the rest of this brief chapter.

Thinking regretfully about the things you do not have, not only is the easiest way to be unhappy, but also is the one cause of unhappiness which is most easily cured. So, since most of us have this unhappy habit to some extent, let's get on with the easy cure.

Limit your wants. Cut down your wants to the barest essentials. Be acutely conscious that you do not *really need,* you do not *really want,* but a very *few* absolutely essential things—which you already have or can readily obtain. Eddie Rickenbacker with his companions drifted in life rafts, hopelessly lost in the Pacific Ocean for 21 days. When asked what was the biggest lesson he learned from this ordeal of terrible suffering, he said: "If you have all the fresh water you want to drink and all the food you want to eat, you ought never complain about anything."

Does this mean you have to be satisfied with a life consisting only of fresh water and enough food? Certainly not. But it does suggest that you can avoid unhappiness and attain happiness by confining what will make you contented and happy to the fewest possible necessary things—*then* everything else desirable which you obtain will *add* to your happiness. It's just as simple as that.

Thus you can go through life adding something —perhaps a lot of things—to your happiness every day. Every good thing you do or get—no matter how little—will add to your happiness. You will be increasingly happy, because you not only will possess what you have decided you *really* need, but you will have a *happiness bonus* in all the additional good things you acquire as you daily try to improve—without the unhappy pressure of urgent need.

Then imprint your happiness for the abundance of your blessings visibly upon your personality by being grateful. Count your blessings—not your unfilled wants. Count your blessings with such mental and emotional emphasis that your personality becomes radiant with the sheer joy of being alive!

Count your blessings because psychologists consider this to be the easiest and most effective of all mental, emotional and physical therapies.

Count your blessings, not just before you go to sleep at night and as soon as you awake in the morning, but during the many brief intervals of each day's living.

Count your blessings. Be deeply grateful for them. Be radiantly joyful because of them.

Count your blessings—gratefully—for they are the divine gifts of Life to YOU.

Chapter 22

The Epidemic Of Hate

It is an inspiration to see a community—and sometimes an entire nation—unite to ward off or to alleviate an epidemic disease. The mobilization of all necessary resources is effected with urgency and total disregard of cost. There is an all-pervading selfless sacrifice.

Recently, in Britain, because of an epidemic of hoof-and-mouth disease, 450,000 fine cattle were destroyed by their owners. Entire herds representing almost the total assets of thousands of cattlemen were slaughtered and destroyed at a total loss.

Everywhere, throughout the world, epidemics ranging from malaria or typhoid to measles or mumps are put down with organized urgency. Cost is no consideration. Sacrifices are routine and universal. Massive assistance pours in from surrounding, and even distant, communities. If the epidemic is of sufficient magnitude, other nations, including so-called unfriendly ones, send aid.

But all this urgency, this sympathetic assistance, this total disregard of cost, seems to apply only to epidemics of physical disease.

What about epidemics of mental-emotional-spiritual disease?

This nation—and the entire world—is engulfed in an epidemic of hate. If we knew as much about mental health as we know about physical health, we would consider an epidemic of hate to be as dangerous as an epidemic of malaria or typhoid.

First, let us be sure we are not setting up a straw man with which to joust. Is there really an epidemic of hate abroad in the world?

The evidence is conclusive. The supporting facts are clear—and everywhere. We are not approaching a crisis—we are in the midst of one. An epidemic of hate!

Hate is not a physical disease. It is a mental-emotional-spiritual disease and must be treated as such. The physical damage is the result, not the disease, itself; yet most proposed cures would treat the physical results of the epidemic of hate and not its mental-emotional-spiritual causes.

One of the problems is that there is not just one hate, but an all-pervading complex of different hates, interwoven in the fabric of our lives. Each hate has a different cause, which requires a different cure. The hate of one group is the exact opposite of the hate of a different and, perhaps, opposite group.

And there we find a basic cause which may provide a partial beginning for a cure. It is in the confrontation of different and opposite groups (or individuals). Hate is spawned in the very fact of their being different and opposite. There is a natural predisposition for this to occur, and knowing this fact leads toward partial solutions of the problem.

There are three obvious solutions to the hate which results because individuals, groups or nations are different and, to a substantial degree, opposite:

(1) Know that being different and opposite does not always, and need not ever, cause hate.

(2) Seek, recognize and emphasize similarities.

(3) Tolerate differences.

Those three actions would at least provide a beginning toward de-escalating the epidemic of hate which now so completely engulfs us.

But it would be only a beginning. There are so many hates, for so many reasons, among so many individuals, groups and nations, that this brief chapter can only point out the existence of their epidemic proportions and the seriousness of the result. Since it is the purpose of this book only to provide the subject matter for stimulated thought and to encourage each reader to pursue such thoughts to his own conclusions, it is proper to leave this problem with you for you to think about and to act upon to the extent you choose. And so I turn it over to you—with this final suggestion:

An epidemic of hate cannot exist in an atmosphere of good will. Perhaps our first task must be the creation—somehow—or a deep, sincere, all-pervading atmosphere of good will among all individuals, groups and nations.

You will recall hearing that this thought was expressed before—some 2,000 years ago. It promised then, as it does now, that when there is good will among men, we shall have peace on earth.

Chapter 23

The Gentle Art Of Letting Alone

Having retired at the rather early age of fifty so that I could devote my full time to helping others, I have undertaken numerous projects, which it is not the purpose of this book to describe—except one, which follows.

I have been interested in exploring the question of why people—almost all of us—get involved in so much unpleasantness, so many problems, so much trouble. It seems to be a natural human failing.

I started by analyzing, insofar as I could remember, my own past propensity for becoming involved in unpleasantness, problems and all sorts of difficulties, small, medium and large. To my own half-century of trouble-involvement, I added that of many other people whom I have known or read about. So my "sample", as researchers would call it, was quite large and adequately diversified—at least sufficient to provide some helpful conclusions which I now would like to share with you.

First, let us concede that there are a number of dedicated trouble-makers among us who for various psychological reasons, are *impelled* to cause trouble. Later, in this chapter, we shall discuss how to deal with them.

But it is the inadvertent trouble-involvement of the rest of us which we principally want to consider now.

After considerable study of this strange phenomenon, it turns out that, in most cases—*all avoidable*—we, ourselves, are the culprits! We unintentionally and inadvertently do, say or write things which are the subsequent causes of our own troubles. Or we unnecessarily escalate potential trouble into real trouble. And often we persist in an action-reaction sequence which not only maintains our trouble-involvement, but increases it.

We haven't learned the GENTLE ART OF LETTING ALONE.

In most cases—*all avoidable*—we initiate our own troubles by two actions: (1) Unnecessary involvement or, much worse, *over*-involvement, and (2) Unnecessary reaction or, much worse, *over*-reaction. Let us briefly examine both of these methods by which we unnecessarily and inadvertently cause ourselves trouble.

(1) Unnecessary involvement or over-involvement:

It is not necessary that we join every conflict, take sides in every cause (especially controversial causes) and thus gain an additional supply of enemies. Yes, admittedly, we may also gain some friends, but the enemies made in controversy seem to remain long after the friends we made have faded into acquaintances. Anyway, there are many quicker, easier, better ways to make friends. But there are few quicker, easier, better ways make enemies.

We should use the GENTLE ART OF LETTING ALONE.

Over-involvement in too many causes diffuses our time, dissipates our energies and disorganizes our lives. We do not have to accept every task, shoulder every responsibility, assume every burden which may .be offered us or even thrust upon us. We must do as recommended in Chapter 19: PUSH OUR WHEELBARROW UPSIDE DOWN or people will throw their burdens into it, thus making them *our* burdens. If we go about, collecting burdens at random, we shall soon break under their weight.

Nobody made us General Manager of the Universe and we do not have to accept the responsibilities of personally solving many, if any, of its vast problems. Nor are we required to worry about how others (who have been elected, selected or employed for such purpose) manage situations which only remotely affect us, if at all. Certainly, we should not plunge physically or even mentally into every crisis which does not involve us. There will be enough which do.

We need to learn and to practice the GENTLE ART OF LETTING ALONE.

Now, how about the other way in which we initiate our own troubles?

(2) Unnecessary reaction or *over*-reaction:

Almost everybody has a built-in instinct to react. Human reaction is not always a cause of trouble.

It can be the cause of much happiness. Human reaction runs the full scale from the highest degree of ecstasy to the most violent degree of hatred.

We shall confine our discussion here only to some of the trouble-escalating forms of reaction and over-reaction—especially to our responses when *our feeling of importance* (real or imagined) is demeaned or attacked. Our natural instinct is to react in defense of our feeling of importance, using such weapons as we think appropriate, ranging from sarcastic, insulting, or threatening responses (written or oral or even implied) to physical attack (overt or subversive).

Thus WE escalate trouble, and if we *over-react*, we magnify it at the same time.

Our adversary then becomes our enemy and in turn, reacts or over-reacts accordingly. What started as a spark is fanned into a blaze which becomes a serious fire and finally an inferno.

Why?

Because WE unnecessarily reacted or, worse, *over*-reacted.

The way to prevent escalation of trouble is not to escalate it *yourself*. Just because somebody starts the fire of trouble you don't have to pour gasoline on it! In fact, you will do better to do nothing. Then it will remain your adversary's fire to burn his own fingers in the tending.

The best reaction to would-be trouble-makers is to completely ignore them. Nothing is more defusing to another's explosive temper than total indifference. As a response to an affront, indifference is much more effective than indignation. It turns the quarrel off. There cannot be a one-person quarrel. But be sure that your indifference is genuine. You must really feel indifferent, both for your own tranquility and to be able to express your indifference with disarming non-response. Counting to 10 or to 10,000 while you are seething inwardly, will do little good. You must so genuinely ignore the matter that it obviously is too inconsequential for *you* even to notice.

Never react or over-react in anger. If you do not become involved, you cannot escalate a quarrel. Completely ignore it.

The way to avoid most troubles is to apply the GENTLE ART OF LETTING ALONE.

And, specifically, which situations should you LET ALONE?

Here are two of many examples.

Use this simple test. Ask yourself these questions:

If you would carry out the action considered:

(a) Would you threaten to cause LOSS? Any threat invites antagonistic response, but the threat of LOSS provokes instant hostility. People will *compete* for gain, but they will *fight* to avoid loss. Never do, say or write anything which threatens to cause loss to another. LET IT ALONE!

(b) Would you belittle another's feeling of importance? This chapter has warned against *your* reacting offensively to such a situation, but the odds are that another will respond with often a surprising degree of antagonism to any demeaning of *his* precious feeling of importance. If you cannot *add* to another's feeling of importance—LET IT ALONE!

These are but two of many examples of situations to which you should apply the GENTLE ART OF LETTING ALONE.

It would be constructive and rewarding for you to complete the list for yourself.

Chapter 24

Save For Your Old Age! : MEMORIES!!!

It is one of the first essentials of prudent self-management to save financially for your retirement years. Save money regularly. Keep it safely.

But saving *money* for your old age is *not* enough.

Save pleasant *memories* too! Lots of them! And keep them safely, because you'll need them as much as money—when the inevitable time comes that you cannot see very far forward, but can see a long way back.

Saving pleasant memories can make all the difference between sunset years of happiness, and gloomy, saddened years of regret.

So start your own MEMORY BANK. Keep in your Memory Bank all of your happy memories and make regular deposits of additional pleasant memories. Deliberately build a big reserve of happy memories—and don't keep a debit of unhappy memories which will cancel out the happy ones.

Here's how to start and operate your own MEMORY BANK:

(1) Start now. Today! Don't put it off another day.

(2) Keep a *written* record of your pleasant memories, supplemented by photographs, picture post cards, descriptive folders, menus of outstanding restaurants where you have dined, even match-book covers and other mementos. Don't depend on your memory. You'll surely forget dates, names, places—even entire events. And you will forget increasingly as you grow older, which is exactly when you will have the most time and the most need for all the happy memories you can acquire. The best way to keep all this miscellaneous assortment of notes, folders, menus, and other mementos is in a scrapbook. Not in a file. Files are excellent for segregating papers by dates and subjects—but the joy of a scrapbook Memory Bank is in the browsing and the little surprises of discovering again some happy event of the past which you had forgotten.

(3) Go back over your past—*now*—and retrieve, note down and paste in your Memory Bank scrapbook all the happy occasions you can remember. Don't delay. Your happy memories are golden. They are much too valuable to trust to a human mind, the capacity of which to recall past events fades with every passing day.

(4) Then keep your *written* deposits in your Memory Bank up to date. Don't let them accumulate again until it becomes a project. Keep the feeling that making a

memory deposit in your Memory Bank is more important (and more lasting) than making a money deposit in your bank.

(5) *Make* memories! This is probably the most important and rewarding thing you ever will do. Before you can deposit money in your bank, you first must make that money. So it is with memories. Before you can make a written memory deposit in your Memory Bank, you first must *make* that memory. Often memory material just happens, but you have to be alert to remember, record and deposit it in your Memory Bank scrapbook—promptly.

But it's more fun to consciously and deliberately *make* memories that you will want to keep and treasure throughout the years. Here's how:

(a) Go to interesting, unusual and memorable places. Take photographs, save picture post cards, folders, mementos. Put them in your Memory Bank scrapbook promptly. And be sure to *date* them. I learned that from actual experience. I've been to lots of interesting and memorable places, but because I failed to keep a record of dates, I can't remember *when* I went where! It may not seem important at the time, but in later years you'll find yourself wondering, "Now, just *when* was that?"

(b) Do interesting, unusual and memorable things. It may seem inconvenient, foolish or foolhardy at the time; it may require physical or social courage—but if it will *make* a memory to keep a lifetime in your Memory Bank—*do* it! Then you can say, "The time I rode that elephant . . . " or, "When I went down the rapids of Snake River on a rubber raft . . . " or, "When I asked the Sultan if he spoke English . . . " or just, "The best steak I ever ate was in an out-of-the-way little restaurant in . . . " or even, "When I wrote the Senator about that, he wrote me . . . ."

(c) *Meet* and *talk* with interesting and memorable people. (Make a note of it in your Memory Bank scrapbook—with the *date.*) It is *easy* to meet and talk with interesting and memorable people. In fact, this is the one of the quickest and easiest ways to make memories to put in your Memory Bank.

There are so many methods of starting conversations that they would fill a book. Since that isn't the subject or purpose of this book, there isn't space to go into detail, but here is just one of many easy, effective methods of meeting and talking with interesting and memorable people: Simply walk up to each of them and courteously say, "Mr. Blank, I understand that you are an authority on (name of subject). I would greatly appreciate your telling me if (question that can be answered briefly)." You can continue your conversation if the time and situation seem appropriate. Whether you have a brief or a long discussion, you will have accomplished your purpose, which is to *meet* and *talk* with an interesting, memorable person. You will have done that even if the other person discourteously (which is very unlikely) tells you to go jump in the lake! What an amusing item for your Memory Bank!

(d) If you can't meet and talk with interesting and memorable people, *write* to them. Be sure to write personal complimentary letters which require a (preferably brief) reply. Just writing letters of commendation in the hope that you will receive a courteous acknowledgment, will produce too meager material for your Memory Bank. Always write for a reply which will give you information or an opinion. Then you'll have, not only an interesting Memory Bank deposit, but useful conversational material. Important people are accustomed to, and staffed for, answering mail, so you'll almost certainly get an answer to a properly written question. Here's a simple outline to follow:

Start with a sincere and deserved compliment. Ask an intelligent, thought-provoking question on a subject upon which the person you write is a known (or presumed) authority. Be sure your question can be answered *briefly* and does not require time-consuming research. Have a good reason for *needing* the answer and state your reason briefly. Express gratitude in advance. Do *not* give the impression that you intend this to be the beginning of a continuing, extended exchange of correspondence. Busy people do not want to become involved with perennial letter-writers.

Memory Banks are much too personal and private for public exposure, except to provide interesting bits of conversation on occasion. By their very nature they contain too much ego-involvement and I shall not bore you by turning this chapter into an autobiography under the pretext of furnishing an example.

In return for such considerations, I beg you to do one thing—not for me—but for yourself. Start your own Memory Bank *now*. Keep a written record of your pleasant memories, supplemented by photographs, picture post cards, descriptive folders, menus of outstanding restaurants where you have dined, even match-book covers and other mementos. Keep these in a big scrapbook where you can browse at random, recalling the happy events of the past which the flight of years otherwise would have erased.

Then consciously, deliberately, *make* pleasant memories which you can deposit frequently in your scrapbook Memory Bank. *Go* to interesting, unusual, memorable places. *Do* interesting, unusual, memorable things. *Meet* and *talk* with interesting and memorable people. Or *write* to them with a question on the subject on which each is an authority.

By doing those things you will *make* many pleasant memories to enjoy as you travel life's way. Most important of all, you will store up treasures to count again and again during those long, vacant hours which too often make up our later years. Your own Memory Bank will turn empty old age into a full, joyous sunset of life!

Chapter 25

How YOU Can Radiate Personal Magnetism Like Movie And T.V. Stars

Except for "character" actors who specialize in portraying unpleasant, anti-social parts, the real stars of movies and television are those who radiate personal magnetism.

Since this is the secret of their attraction of other people, not only on stage, but in public (and intimately), it is obvious that radiating personal magnetism is a technique which surely should be used by everyone who wants to be popular and successful. You can do it as easily and as well as any famous personality if you are willing to devote the next few minutes to learning how to do it—and then practicing in all those little wasted spaces in life when you wonder what there is interesting to do.

First, it is well to know that in those fields of endeavor which require personal magnetism (and these include most situations involving being with people) the not-too-generally-known information on the next few pages may be of tremendous value. However, if you infrequently associate with others or if you prefer to be drab and uninteresting, you can skip the next few pages and miss the opportunity of being attractive to others *regardless of your age or physical appearance.*

Let's read again those last few words. Being able to radiate personal magnetism has *nothing* whatever to do with your *physical appearance* or your *age*. There are a lot of charming, little old ladies with happy faces wrinkled with smile-lines, who radiate an exciting personal magnetism which makes most swim-suit models mere walking statues by comparison!

So don't count yourself out because of your age or personal appearance. There is nothing you can do about your age—but enjoy it. And there is little you can do about your physical appearance—except improve it from the *inside*, which is what part of this chapter is about. So let's get started:

To use the movie and T.V. star technique of radiating personal magnetism to attract other people requires that you do three things:

(1) Generate an INNER "GLOW".

(2) Radiate an OUTER "GLOW".

(3) SMILE with your EYES!

So . . . how do you (1) Generate an *inner "glow"*? Naturally, you cannot radiate magnetism you haven't got. So how do you get it? The technique of (1) Generating an *inner "glow"* (personal magnetism) is to consciously arouse a feeling which is a combination of alertness, excitement, exhilaration, elation, anticipation, confidence and emotional power. Then be acutely aware of an intensification, a surging build-up of these feelings, while you consciously are keeping this combination of emotions restrained and controlled—but *ready* to release to whatever extent you will. This will produce a vibrant, inner tenseness which has the exciting qualities of the combination of feelings and emotions just described. In this way you generate the *inner "glow"* (personal magnetism) which you can "project" or "radiate" to others.

Frequently practice arousing this combination of feelings within you. First practice while you are alone, preferably in a quiet place where there will be no distractions. Make a written list of the feelings you want to arouse. Write them in the following order on a small card or piece of paper. Then practice . . . practice . . . practice:

Alertness . . . excitement . . . exhilaration . . . elation . . . anticipation . . . confidence . . . emotional power!

Intensify each feeling—one at a time:

First, feel ALERT! Feel a keen sense of awareness of yourself and your surroundings. Feel watchful . . . ready to act . . . ready to respond—instantly!

Then feel a sense of EXCITEMENT! Come alive! Feel a thrill running through your nervous system! Breathe a little faster!

Now, feel EXHILARATED! Give yourself an emotional lift! Step up your emotional charge!

Then feel ELATED! Get that "sitting-on-top-of-the-world" feeling!

Next feel ANTICIPATION! Feel that "something wonderful" is about to happen!

Then feel CONFIDENT! Very confident! Feel that you are going to get what you want! You are going to do what you want to do! You are *sure* of yourself! *Absolutely sure!*

Finally, feel a sense of EMOTIONAL POWER! Know that you can make *others* feel your emotional power! That you can *radiate* your emotional power! That your emotional power surrounds you like an aura! That anyone near you can feel it *intensely!*

Practice arousing these emotional feelings within yourself. Begin by practicing them one at a time—in the order given. Then see how *intensely* you can feel each one. Next hold the first feeling while you add another . . . and another . . . and another. Finally you will be able to combine ALL of these feelings into *one powerful feeling of personal magnetism!*

Now, you must learn the secret of *maintaining* and *using* personal magnetism!

Having aroused the emotions just listed, you must make them *magnetic* by consciously restraining them and deliberately keeping them under your personal control. It is this conscious *restraint,* this deliberate *control,* that generates the *intensity* of feeling which produces *personal magnetism.* It is the deliberate maintaining of this inner tenseness which produces *magnetic power.* It is the conscious personal control which enables you to direct this *magnetic power*—when, where, and to what extent you choose.

You now have learned step (1) of the *personal magnetism* secret of the movie and television stars and all other magnetic personalities: (1) Generate an INNER "GLOW".

Now for step (2) of their secret, which is: (2) Radiate an OUTER "GLOW".

Since you have learned to (1) Generate an *inner "glow"*, it is quite easy to radiate it outward, to project it to others. You simply develop the "feeling" of doing so. You "feel" that you are surrounded by an aura of *radiant* personal magnetism—just as a real magnet is surrounded by what is known in science as a "magnetic field". You develop the conscious feeling that you can *attract* anything you want within your "magnetic field".

Practice the powerful technique of *projecting* your magnetic personality to others. Practice the "feel" of being able to *radiate* your *inner "glow"* so that it surrounds you with an *outer "glow"* that is your own *magnetic field* which *influences* and *attracts* others.

Once you have (1) Generated an INNER "GLOW", you'll find it easy to be able to project it and thus (2) Radiate an OUTER "GLOW". In fact, if you have intensely generated an *inner "glow"*, it naturally and automatically will radiate as an *outer "glow"*.

So now we come to the third step in the three-part secret of personal magnetism: (3) SMILE with your EYES.

Most people think that they should smile with their mouths. If you try to start a smile with your mouth, it will give you a phoney, superficial look. Try it in front of a mirror—and see yourself as others see you!

A genuine, sincere smile starts from *within* you—not from a fixed position of your lips. You have to "feel" a smile before you can express it—and when you do start to express a smile, personality experts have found that you *must* start to smile with your *eyes!*

Try *that* in front of a mirror! First sincerely, inwardly *feel* like smiling. Then smile with your *eyes!* Imagine a humorous twinkle in your eyes. Then intensify it until your eyes are smiling. Yes, you can actually smile with your eyes! You can even laugh with your eyes! This isn't some new and surprising discovery of mine. It has been taught for years by just about all "personality trainers" from success counselors to dramatic schools to song writers. (Remember the old song, "When Irish EYES Are Smiling"?)

The psychological reason for starting your smile, first from the inside, and then from your eyes, is very simple. Whenever you consciously try to express an emotion (unless you have had years of continuous, professional training as an actor or actress) you become self-conscious. You look positively silly trying to "emote" even such a simple expression as a smile with your lips. So you avoid that self-conscious lip expression just by not thinking about your lips at all. As a matter of fact, you don't think about any of your facial expression at all. You just "feel" like smiling and you start expressing that pleasant feeling with your eyes.

Here's what happens (and you can check this in your mirror): As soon as you "feel" inwardly like smiling and start expressing that pleasant feeling with a humorous twinkle in your *eyes,* your entire facial expression changes—in a completely *natural* manner—without any conscious effort on your part at all!

Your "smile lines" wrinkle automatically around your eyes. Your eyes, themselves, brighten and become more intense (and, incidentally, more interesting). Your lips relax and the corners of your mouth turn upward. Your cheeks lift, as does the entire expression of your face. All this happens in a matter of seconds—and without any self-conscious forcing on your part. You instantly have a natural, pleasant, radiant, good-humored expression.

This usually is adequate, sufficient—and generally preferable for most occasions. However, if you feel like it and if the situation is appropriate, just keep going into a big, broad, friendly smile. But once you part your lips and show your teeth, you've got to go all the way to a *big,* broad smile. If you open your lips to smile and only smile half-way, you'll have a self-conscious, simpering smirk.

The safest and best rule is to sincerely *inwardly* feel like smiling . . . then start by *smiling with your eyes* . . . and let nature take it from there.

So, if you want to radiate personal magnetism like movie and television stars, and like the big personality successes in all walks of life:

(1) Generate an INNER "GLOW"
(2) Radiate an OUTER "GLOW"
(3) SMILE with your EYES!

Chapter 26

Be Your Own Ghost

One of the best methods of self-improvement and disciplined effort is to become your own ghost.

This is no hocus-pocus pseudo-psychology. This is one of the simplest and easiest-to-use, practical psychological techniques for self-improvement yet developed. It will produce instant improvement in just about any life activity to which you apply it.

So, be your own ghost. Haunt yourself into self-improvement. Here's how it's done:

You just imagine—visualize—the "real you" stepping outside your own body and standing aside, nearby, watching yourself (critically) as you perform each daily activity.

Visualize this technique until you get it very clearly fixed in your mind. You stand aside from your own physical body . . . detached . . . impartial . . . carefully watching and critically studying how well you do each task.

Of course, this is simply "detached, objective self-analysis". But you'll enjoy it more—and get better results—if you use your imagination to become your own ghost to stand outside yourself and see yourself as others see you.

The whole idea is to critically watch yourself perform each daily task to see if you are doing it as perfectly as possible.

For example, your telephone rings. You watch yourself—through your ghost—to see if you answer your phone with a cheerful "hello" or if you sound irritated at the interruption. Your ghost is watching to see if you mentally "broadcast goodwill" to the other person throughout the entire telephone conversation. Are you speaking with a smile in your voice? Do you give your caller the pleasant impression that his or her phone call is appreciated, and do you express your appreciation in the form of sincere compliments? Your ghost is watching, listening—critically, objectively—and will let you know how well you performed this simple, but important, task of making each telephone call an *event,* not an incident.

Make a pal of your ghost. After all, your ghost is YOU—and if you can't have friendly relations with yourself, you'll never have friendly relations with anybody else. So ask your ghost (mentally, of course): "How did I do?" "How could I have done better?" "What do I need to learn, to practice, in order to improve my performance?" Talk it over (again, mentally, of course) with your ghost. Remember that your ghost has been watching you with critical detachment—from the outside, as others do.

But will not developing the feeling that your ghost is standing nearby, critically watching you perform each daily task, give you a feeling of self-consciousness? Frankly, yes. But it will be a beneficial self-consciousness —not the kind that causes embarrassment, awkwardness, fear, panic.

And exactly what is "beneficial self-consciousness"? It is deliberate purpose, definite objective, controlled action. It is planned, conscious self-improvement. It is not aiming in the general direction of your target—it is consciously, deliberately, aiming directly, accurately, expertly at your target.

This is the purpose of being your own ghost: to stand aside and watch with calm, detached objectivity, your own performance of your daily tasks, with direct aim at self-improvement.

It is a psychological technique which is simple, beneficial and a lot of fun!

Chapter 27

A Wall And Two Roads

When Robert Frost, my favorite poet, was asked to explain one of his poems, he replied, "What do you want me to do—say it over in worser English?"

Such language! And from one of the men who used our language best of all.

No, Mr. Frost, we don't want you to say it over in worser English. But I want to say it over. Not that you didn't make it clear, but because it needs repeating again and again. Besides, I am much more experienced in saying things in worser English than you were.

Now that poem you wrote about a wall . . .

You said, "Before I built a wall, I'd ask to know what I was walling in and walling out. Something there is that doesn't love a wall, that wants it down."

And your neighbor replied that: "Good fences make good neighbors."

I've been wondering about that. Did the Great Wall of China make good neighbors? Did the Maginot Line in France—a sort of inverted wall, built down instead of up—make good neighbors? Did the Berlin Wall make good neighbors?

Then I've been wondering about my own wall. You see, I live in Cherokee Gardens—a beautiful place where it would be highly improper to build a wall of brick or stone. So we build walls of tall, green, flowering shrubs. Gives us "privacy," you know. I can relax outdoors in the warm sun and read or write books without the distraction of seeing children at play or their little puppy dogs trotting from somewhere to nowhere, and back again.

Of course I can hear the children's voices and laughter—but I never quite find out who gets to be Batman and who is Robin. And I can't see where Hunter (that's a dog) hides the bones I put outside my wall for him.

So, Mr. Frost, I can understand why, in your poem, you couldn't quite agree with your neighbor who firmly insisted, "Good fences make good neighbors." With you, I wonder *do* they?

Then, Mr. Frost, there is that poem you wrote about the "two roads" which "diverged in a yellow wood" . . .

Being only "one traveler, long you stood and looked down each as far as you could" . . . then you took one—as each of us must when we are so often faced in Life with the choice between two roads, knowing, as you did, that "we shall never come back."

Yes, Mr. Frost, all of us direct our own lives by our choice of roads. It is a choice we frequently must make. And each choice is important, too, because, as you said, "knowing that way leads on to way . . ." our decision is irrevocable.

How careful we must be in choosing our roads, because some day we shall look back on all those choices and say with you . . .

"THAT has made ALL the difference!"

Chapter 28

"Press On!"

History has not yet decided in which niche to place the marble bust of President Calvin Coolidge. His life is still too close to put in proper perspective. It is as if history were holding his bust as a giant chessman, uncertain where to place it on the chessboard of eternity.

And we, ourselves, haven't thought much about Calvin Coolidge lately, because we are still caught up in the excitement of the youthful enthusiasm of a John Kennedy whose ideas and ideals were cut short of the depth of full maturity and transferred, in a blinding flash of national shock, to Lyndon Johnson, to be replaced in turn, by Richard Nixon then Gerald Ford and James Carter and Ronald Reagan as each sought his place in history.

In the case of Calvin Coolidge, let us thoughtfuly consider what he said, even as we await the final judgment of history on what he did.

One thing we know. Calvin Coolidge thought clearly and precisely before he spoke. And then he spoke with a brevity which was notable. As in the case of his presidential portrait. When it was hung, he and a companion viewed it descerningly and at great length, during which neither spoke a word. Then President Coolidge turned to his friend and quietly said, "I think so, too."

Many people do not know that the President who seldom spoke, made one of the wisest statements of all time. President Coolidge said, "Nothing in the world will take the place of persistence. Talent will not; nothing is more common than unsuccessful men with talent. Genius will not; unrewarded genius is almost a proverb. Education alone will not; the world is full of educated derelicts. Persistence and determination alone are omnipotent. The slogan 'Press on!' has solved and always will solve the problems of the human race."

That statement, alone, should assure President Coolidge's place in history. It should be memorized by every high-school graduate as a prerequisite to graduating. If every high school graduate knew that persistence and determination *alone* are omnipotent, and that the slogan 'Press on!' has solved and always will solve the problems of the human race —how direct the way to achievement would be!

How much better it would be to teach that statement of inspiration and fact by President Coolidge, than to teach the statement made by his famous predecessor that "All men are created equal", a preposterous conclusion, which, in the unlikely event you haven't found it out for yourself, any anthropologist will tell you just isn't so.

How much better it is to know that, while by natural process you haven't been created equal—you still can, by persistence and determination *alone* attain a measure of value, and "Press on!" to become not merely equal, but *superior!*

Little good and much harm have come from unfounded illusions of equality—but almost everything good has come from persistence and determination.

Equality does not come by natural process, nor can equality result from environment, nor can equality be bestowed by some benevolent government. Equality must be *earned* by persistent and determined effort—by "pressing on" to *individual* achievement.

And nobody need stop when he or she merely has earned equality—because simply by continuing the same persistence and determination, simply by "pressing on", *superiority* can be attained.

Here in the United States, in this land of freedom to achieve to the full extent of one's ability, persistence and determination—neither equality nor superiority is limited by race, color or creed. Examples are everywhere! So let no one say that it cannot be done. Because it *has* been done! And it *is* being done every day!

It is greatly to be regretted that so many people have been misled into devoting their energies to demanding equality as a *right*—when those same energies could have earned equality or superiority as an *achievement*.

The way to attain that achievement is the way President Calvin Collidge said "has solved and always will solve the problems of the human race." And note that he said "*human* race"—not any specific race. So, let's sit before that quiet, thoughtful President and again listen carefully as he says:

"Nothing in the world will take the place of persistence. Talent will not; nothing is more common than unsuccessful men with talent. Genius will not; unrewarded genius is almost a proverb. Education alone will not; the world is full of educated derelicts. Persistence and determination alone are omnipotent. The slogan 'Press on!' has solved and always will solve the problems of the human race."

When history gets around to placing that marble bust of Calvin Coolidge in its niche among the world's great, I hope it places him up among the high and mighty, because in his concise, terse way, he told *how* they became high and mighty—so that we, too, could become equal or superior.

Chapter 29

How To Avoid Or Get Rid Of Resentment

Resentment is one of the most prevalent and dangerous emotional ills that befalls us (or perhaps I should more accurately say: "that we bring upon ourselves").

Here is what the psychologists say about resentment:

Resentment is an attempt to excuse (to others or to ourselves) our own failure by attributing it to injustice or unfair treatment by those resented. Habitual resentment turns inward in the form of self-pity that becomes a chronic emotional agony which seeks relief in the sympathy and servitude of others.

There are no more unpleasant companions than those whose resentment has turned to self-pity. They feel that others should be dedicated, no matter at what inconvenience, to providing them with physical, mental and especially emotional, well-being. They expect (and inwardly demand) undying gratitude for favors, attentions or services, even the most insignificant, which they may have rendered others in the past. They feel that these "debts" which others "owe" them must be paid, again and again, in sympathy, attention and services, and their resentment spreads to include these "debtors" if such "debts" are not repeatedly paid and repaid.

Thus begins one phase of resentment: self-pity, which is the cause of much chronic emotional agony and much mental absorption in negative thinking.

But self-pity is just one of the results of resentment. There is another in which resentment begins with burning anger and escalates through an upward spiral to hatred, vengeance, and sometimes murder or insanity. Usually resentment escalates to intense feelings of hatred, often to a conscious or subconscious desire for vengeance, sometimes fulfilled by action.

Much too often does the resentment-hatred-vengeance spiral culminate in murder. While vengeance is not the only motive for murder (although it often is a principal ingredient), and while firearms are not the only means of murder, it is a shocking statistic that since 1900 more than 750,000 Americans have been shot to death in their homes, which far exceeds all of the Americans killed in battle in all the wars in which the United States has fought.

Even though murder and insanity are unlikely climaxes for the feelings of resentment which most of us experience all too frequently, resentment causes so much emotional tension, irritation and often severe anguish that all of us should:

(1) Learn to avoid resentment.

(2) Get rid of any and all feelings of resentment which we now have (yes, even that pet resentment we almost enjoy).

It clearly is not intended that this book presume to be even a partial text on psychology—nor a complete text on any subject. It is merely a book containing, as its name describes: "Thoughts To Build On". Its purpose is to be a thought-starter, to stimulate interesting and, I hope, constructive thoughts, some of which you may want to explore further in more comprehensive texts on those subjects.

So, within the limitations of the purpose of this book, let's think about resentment . . . how to avoid it . . . and how to get rid of it if it already is in your emotional complexes.

Let's start by understanding exactly what resentment really is.

Resentment is an emotional reliving of an unpleasant happening of the past. Knowing what resentment actually is, should help us learn to avoid it, or, having previously failed to avoid it, learn to get rid of it. More precisely, resentment is our unfavorable reaction to what we consider to be an affront to our precious egos or an attack on our person, relationships or belongings.

Since resentment is a reaction to something unpleasant which has happened, how do we put a block between the unpleasant happening and our reaction to it in the form of resentment? In various ways, and here are a few:

IGNORE it! The cultivated art of being able to ignore real or imagined unpleasant past happenings will save you much unnecessary anguish. The past is done. You cannot change the past no matter how many times you re-live it in memory. So why suffer the re-living of unpleasant past experiences? Since you cannot change them—*ignore* them and *forget* them.

"More easily said than done", you may reply. And, if you are a particularly sensitive person, your excuse is partially true. Are your "feelings" easily hurt? Are you overly sensitive to what others say or do, so that you take offense at the least word or action which does not flatter your precious ego? Are you "thin-skinned" emotionally so that the slightest social "cut" is a deep and painful wound? Then here are some proven, helpful suggestions:

GET TOUGH emotionally. Be like tough General Smedley Butler, when he was commanding general of the U. S. Marines. "Old Hell-Devil Butler", they called him. And that wasn't the only name they called him, either! He said he had been called every unprintable name in the book. He had been cussed by experts. How did he react? Did he feel hurt? Was he offended? Did he smolder in resentment? Not Smedley Butler! He said, "Whenever I hear someone cussing me, I never bother to turn my head to see who's talking."

"Yes", you say, "But General Butler was a tough Marine and I'm just a tender, shrinking violet." O.K., Violet, it's time you got over being tender—and stopped shrinking. And you don't have to be a Marine General to do it.

You can be an elderly, quiet, courteous, distinguished gentleman like Bernard Baruch, who calmly and wisely advised six Presidents. Let wise, thoughtful Bernard Baruch advise you, too. He said, "No man can humiliate or disturb me. I won't let him." That's how to block out resentment before it upsets you emotionally. Just don't *let* anyone humiliate or disturb you.

Your physical body has a built-in "thermostat" which maintains an even body-temperature of 98.6 degrees no matter whether the temperature outside your body is below freezing or a sweltering 120 degrees. Consciously hold "mental pictures" before your subconscious mind, visualizing yourself as having an "emotional thermostat" which maintains your emotions at a pleasant, even "emotional temperature" of relaxed, undisturbed serenity—no matter how frigid the snubs or how heated the personal attacks you inevitably will encounter from time to time. Just simply do not respond nor react to the emotional storms swirling about you, but be as emotionally unconcerned as "the ticking of a clock during a thunderstorm".

Another way to avoid developing feelings of resentment is to adopt the life motto of the great French philosopher, Montaigne: "A man is not hurt so much by *what* happens as by his *opinion* of what happens." Don't make a mountain of resentment out of the molehill of some snub or irritation. Don't "bleed" emotionally from every insulting "cut". If somebody tries to do a "hatchet job" on you, don't let the hatchet make even a dent in your composure and disposition.

Remember, your resentment doesn't hurt the person against whom you harbor the resentment. It hurts only you. So why deliberately hurt yourself? Mentally punching pin-holes in some other person's picture doesn't hurt him or her the least bit—and, sooner or later, you will stick yourself. If you can't love your enemies, at least love yourself enough that you won't let your enemies control your happiness, your disposition and your health.

So, when a resentment-situation arises—*ignore* it and *forget* it. Don't take yourself too seriously—and don't take other people and the irritating things they sometimes do, too seriously, either. Just think of something else. Your mind cannot hold two different thoughts at the same time, so concentrate on *anything* but your budding resentment. Keep busy. Lose yourself in work or active play. If resentment insists on intruding, just laugh in its face and mentally say to it, "Go away, boy, I'm busy, don't bother me!" Be too *big* to be resentful.

Adopt the philosophy of our late President Dwight Eisenhower: "Never waste a minute thinking about anyone you don't like."

But suppose a resentment has already taken root. How do you get *rid* of it? You will find that the methods of *avoiding* resentment described on the preceding pages will also help you get *rid* of established resentment. Most people accept their having some resentments as a natural part of life. It is only when they recognize resentments as persistent causes of unhappiness (and worse!) that they determine to rid themselves of their present resentments and to avoid all resentments in the future. So re-read this chapter. It tells you what resentment really is, what unhappiness it can cause you, and how to avoid it. That brings you a long way toward getting rid of whatever resentments you now possess (or perhaps I should say: "now possess you").

But some additional methods are needed if you are to rid yourself of well-established, deeply-rooted resentments.

One requirement is a sympathetic understanding of the persons you resent. Perhaps they were justified (or, at least, they thought so) in doing whatever it was which caused your resentment. I have discovered, by objective and thoughtful analysis, that actions by others which I have most deeply resented and which have caused me the most unhappiness—are actually RE-actions to something I did *first* which aroused *their* antagonism and thus caused them to act as they did, ultimately causing my own resentment. I'll bet, if you honestly and objectively analyze each of your resentments, you, too, will discover that, in many cases, *you* initially *started*, or, at least, you escalated, the events which finally resulted in your harboring the resentments.

In those cases, your resentments have no valid cause to exist and, in the light of understanding, should promptly vanish. Then you need to do one more thing. Since you caused the other person to act as he did because of his own resentment toward you, you need to remove *his* resentment, too. Do this by apologizing, or by directly or indirectly making amends, or by whatever appropriate and effective method is needed to remove *his* resentment of you. Otherwise, if you permit his resentment to exist, he will continue to act toward you in a way which will continue to arouse your resentment. And the vicious cycle will resume.

In many other cases you will find that the slurs, slights, rudeness or other annoyances by which people arouse your resentment are not intentional at all, but are caused by the very human trait of each of us being preoccupied with our own thoughts, plans, problems and affairs. Others probably are not thinking about how radiantly happy it would make you if they greeted you with extremely cordial enthusiasm. I have learned that it makes absolutely no difference whether I am greeted cordially, indifferently, or not at all. I am not running for elective office, nor am I in a popularity contest. And I can always attract others' attention by initiating the conversation or action myself—with the same or better results.

So don't take yourself—or others—too seriously. The unhappy resentments aren't worth it!

Objectively seek understanding of the *origin* of your resentments by looking at them in relation to the total personal problems, ambitions and points-of-view of the persons you now resent. You'll find that from *their* side they may have been justified—or thought they were—in doing what you resent. Then, with the addition of whatever *self*-discipline is required, you'll find that your resentments will fade into the oblivion they justly deserve.

Chapter 30

Don't Attract To You – Go To Them!

Personal magnetism is a very desirable quality. There are great personal benefits to be derived from the ability to attract others to you. I have written a chapter in this book (Chapter 25) explaining how you can use the methods of movie and television stars to develop personal magnetism, yourself. And I do not propose, in this present chapter, to retract what I said in Chapter 25 concerning personal magnetism.

I simply want to point out here that there is another way to influence people favorably—which produces much the same beneficial results as personal magnetism—but which works on an almost opposite principle.

To be specific, using the method I now want to explain, you do not attract people to you—you GO TO THEM!

Western Union used to feature the slogan: "Don't write—TELEGRAPH!" There is much merit in that suggestion and I often have, and still do, recommend it.

Then those of us who trained salesmen and taught management used to emphasize: "Don't write—don't telegraph—*GO!!!*"

There are great advantages in the admonition to . . . *GO!!!*

GO . . . where the business is!

GO . . . where the money is!

GO . . . where the people are!

GO . . . where the action is!

GO . . . where the fun is!

But this chapter isn't about that. This chapter will explain a simple method of getting another person to do what you want him to do. To do this you . . . *GO!* Here is how:

Find out where another's attention is . . . and *go there* with your own conversation. He'll probably think you are the most interesting conversationalist he has ever met—because you are talking directly to *his* attention, exactly where it is focused at that very moment.

Find out where another's interest is . . . and *go there* with your own interest, making your interest one with his. When you take your interest where another's interest is, when you *join* your interests with *his,* you cement an alliance which is mutually unbreakable.

Find out where another's beliefs are . . . and *go there* with your own beliefs. Use your beliefs to endorse, confirm, vindicate *his* beliefs. Combine your beliefs with *his* beliefs. Merge your beliefs with *his* beliefs and you will together build a fortress of mutual belief and he will forever be your ally in defending it.

Find out where another's desires are . . . and *go there* with the exact satisfactions to fulfill *his* desires, fully and completely. You can attain no greater influence than the ability and willingness to fulfill the desires of others . . . exactly . . . completely . . . immediately.

It requires considerable personality training, ability and technique to attain the personal magnetism to attract others to *come to you.* But it requires only willingness and effort to *go to them.* In either case, you reach the same goal—the proximity which permits joining together for your mutual benefit.

For you to accomplish that, by either method, will require the ability on your part to accurately appraise the attention, interests, beliefs and desires of the other person—and to be able and willing to accommodate your own attention, interests, beliefs and desires to *his,* so that you will proceed together in an unbreakable alliance toward a mutually-determined goal.

This proven success-method requires *giving before getting.* It is based on the proven premise that it not only is "better to give than to receive" but it is "*necessary* to give *in order* to receive".

The executive who has a sign on his desk reading, "Be reasonable, do it *my* way", isn't kidding.

The buyer who says, "These are our specifications. Our deadline on bids is two weeks", isn't kidding, either.

Neither is the personnel manager who says,

"Here are the personal qualifications which we require of all applicants for this particular job."

It used to be that the way to succeed was to dominate others, first to pressure, and more recently to influence, people to do things *your* way.

Now, the way to succeed is to cooperatively adjust to the requirements of those upon whom your success depends. You adjust to the direction of *their* attention . . . you adjust to the subject of *their* interests . . . you adjust to re-enforce *their* beliefs . . you adjust to satisfy *their* desires.

Doesn't this make you a will-less, jellyfish of a creature whose only desire is to please? Not at all! It requires more will-power to relinquish your own demands, than it does to try to cram them down somebody else's throat—if you could. It requires more ability to smoothly adjust, than it does to offensively dominate—if you could. It requires more intelligence to cooperate than to be obstructive—if you could.

Please note that the preceding statements are followed by: *"if you could"*. Because the fact is: YOU CANNOT. When you are dealing with people upon whose decisions your success depends: you cannot cram your demands down their throats, you cannot offensively dominate them, you cannot obstruct their chosen paths to their goals. You cannot have *your* way, but you must adjust to *their* way.

That does not mean that, once you are on the team, once you are an *insider,* you cannot make constructive suggestions. In fact, you'll be asked to—and expected to—when you are *"in"*. Then, the more improvements you can suggest, the faster you will succeed.

But I want to briefly review for emphasis:

Attracting people to you is great . . . but *going to them* is faster!

Find out where another's attention is . . . and *go there* with your conversation. Then his attention will turn to you.

Find out where another's interest is . . . and *go there* with your own interest, making your interest one with his. When you *join* your interest with his, you cement an alliance which is mutually unbreakable.

Find out where another's beliefs are . . . and *go there* with your own beliefs which endorse, confirm, vindicate and re-enforce his beliefs. He will be your constant ally in defending them.

Find out what another's desires are . . . and *go there* with the exact satisfactions to fulfill his desires.

You have to *give* before you can *get*.

To be a GO-GETTER, you must first adopt as your life plan, the title of an excellent book . . . and be a GO-GIVER!

Chapter 31

"Be Prepared"

There is much wisdom to be found in mottoes. One of the wisest of all is the motto of the Boy Scouts: "Be Prepared".

The admonition to "Be Prepared" applies to almost every facet of life, and since we cannot examine all in one brief chapter, I'm going to choose perhaps the most unpleasant—but most needed.

Malcolm Muggeridge said, "Religion wisely assumes misfortune, and so survives, when earthly utopian hopes, which must inevitably be disappointed, soon perish".

We should not leave the assumption of misfortune entirely to religion. The acceptance of the inevitability of misfortune, as a frequent or infrequent part of life, should be individual and not a matter of religion only.

So each of us should "Be Prepared" to accept such misfortunes as inevitably will come our way, realizing that life was not made for our enjoyment, but for our living.

Nor is it proper for us to complain; because, in complaining we would, in justice, have to define such of our terms as "misfortune" and "enjoyment".

Would you describe the ultimate in inevitable misfortune as being death—that of a loved one, or yourself? Do you think of life as the ticking of a clock which grows louder with each passing day until it becomes the tolling of a bell? You don't have to ask for whom the bell tolls. You know.

Yet, even as the ticking goes on, you must consider the words of Swift, who wrote: "It is impossible that anything so natural, so necessary, and so universal as death, should ever have been designed by Providence as an evil to mankind."

The ticking reminds us, too, of the words of ın unknown author:

"The clock of life is wound but once,
And no one has the power
To tell just when the hands will stop,
At late or early hour.

"NOW is the only time you own
Live, love, toil with a will;
Place no faith in tomorrow, for
The clock may then be still."

You cannot control the length of your life, but you can control its other dimensions: its breadth, its depth, and its height. It is within these dimensions that you live your unrepeatable miracle, for that's what life is—a miracle . . . and unrepeatable.

Perhaps, life's being a miracle explains our inability to describe its terms. But even if we do not know what "misfortune" is and what it is not, for chameleon-like, it can change from bad to good, depending on how we view it, we would do well to "wisely assume" and "Be Prepared".

Being prepared for the inevitability of what we assume to be misfortune does not mean that we must dwell on it, be preoccupied with it, nor dread its certain coming. We should simply recognize the fact that: "This, too, will change", and be reconciled to that eventuality so that, should the inevitability of change lead to less favorable circumstances, we shall be neither overwhelmed nor even surprised. And being neither overwhelmed nor surprised by misfortune, we shall respond as we have prepared to do, with calm acceptance and serenity.

Thus having prepared for the inevitability of such misfortunes as we shall meet along the way, we can continue our journey through life with poise and confidence.

"To be forewarned is to be forearmed" is not just a physical thing; it is, in the context of this chapter: mental, emotional, and yes, especially, spiritual. To know in advance that "not enjoyment and not sorrow, is our destined end or way", is to "Be Prepared" with a realistic attitude toward life which is not based on the "utopian hopes", which Malcolm Muggeridge warned: "must inevitably be disappointed, soon perish".

So let us be forewarned and therefore forearmed—mentally, emotionally and spiritually—to "meet with triumph and disaster", and as Kipling advised, "treat those two imposters just the same".

Yes, the graph-lines of every life move up and down. In realizing and accepting this, we achieve, in our personality, "The Vital Balance" about which psychiatrist Dr. Karl Menninger wrote. We can "Be Prepared" without being apprehensive—because it is in the serene knowledge of our preparedness that we lose our apprehension and attain that vital balance and composure to meet the inevitable vicissitudes of life.

Chapter 32

TALK! . . . A Way To Success

How you talk . . . what you say . . . to whom you say it, and when . . . may well determine the degree of your success in life.

The foregoing statement is well worth your study—and re-study—because it may be the most important statement in this entire book.

To help you learn, in necessary detail: (1) How to talk . . . (2) What to say . . . (3) To whom to say it . . . (4) When to say it . . . would require an entire book (perhaps an entire set of books), not just this one chapter. So, important as this is to you, we can only consider here a few practical suggestions and hope that you will seek more detailed information from more specialized books.

Let's start with how to talk fluently—because that is essential. And let's start with the most horrible example—me.

I'm using myself as an example for two reasons. First, as a child, I could *not talk at all,* at least not without stammering so incoherently that I could not recite in school and had to be excused from making the then-required high school senior speech. The second reason for using myself as an example is that I know exactly what I did to change from not being able to talk, to being able to talk fluently.

From my own experience, I learned that the way to learn to talk fluently is to *talk*.

In the unlikely event that you must start from the poor beginning that I did, you need to know two important facts of life: (1) Do the thing and you will have the power . . . (2) Start by doing what you can do easily, then progress through easy steps to doing the next most difficult thing.

Since my stammering was caused by self-consciousness, and since most people are, to some extent, self-conscious—you may benefit by reading this brief account of how I cured it.

First: "Do the thing and you will have the power." So I talked . . . and I talked . . .and I talked . . . and I *talked!* How? Simply by using the second precept just described: "Start by doing what you can do easily, then progress through easy steps to doing the next most difficult thing."

In my case, since I stammered, I started by "talking" silently to myself. I went through all the talking impulses and motions, but I deliberately did not make a sound. Since I was alone, I wasn't self-conscious, and since I made no sound, I didn't stammer. Then I whispered. No problem! So I whispered louder . . . and louder . . .

and louder—until I was speaking at (and above) natural volume.

In easy steps, I talked to myself in the mirror, then to individuals, small groups, civic meetings, large audiences, from church pulpits and even from the same speakers' platform with a U. S. cabinet member and, finally, broadcast to the world on the "Voice of America" Radio Program.

So, you can learn to talk fluently (and with much less difficulty than I did) just by *talking*. Talk to anybody, everybody, nearby, about something. Don't make a speech—just a comment. Make your comment casually, easily, with good humor and friendliness.

An unsolicited comment has its own built-in terminal facility. If you do not ask for a reply, you may not get one. So if you want to extend a conversation, ask a question. The first step in opening a conversation with a stranger (or in launching a new subject of conversation with anyone) is to frankly admit that you don't know something. Then say that you want or need to know about it and ask the person you are questioning if he or she can furnish you the information. A noted conversationalist said that, properly asked, there was almost no limit to the time and trouble another would take to further your education.

Since the way to improve your ability to talk fluently, is to engage in conversations with as many different individuals and groups as possible, learn the art of *asking*. It is more accurate, instead of saying, "TALK your way to success", that we say, "ASK your way to success". Here's how you can do it:

(1) ASK others to give you the *information* you need to succeed.

(2) ASK others to *do* what you want them to do to help you succeed.

(3) ASK others to *provide* you with what you you need in order to succeed.

There are proven psychological principles (which are too complex to explain in this brief chapter) that cause people to do what they are properly *asked* to do—if they reasonably can. Of course, everybody cannot or will not do everything you ask—but by the *law of averages*—enough people will do what you properly ask, to make you successful.

Also, concerning what to talk about, now would be a good time to re-read Chapter 20, which describes: "Those Big Signs All Of Us Wear Across Our Chests" . . . invisible signs which read, "I want to be IMPORTANT!" . . . "I want to be ADMIRED!" . . . "I want to be APPRECIATED!" That's what to talk about: the things other people want to hear most—about *themselves*. And be sure to ask leading questions which encourage others to talk about themselves—then *listen*. You'll be surprised at how interested listening eliminates your self-consciousness, furnishes you with the best material with which to continue the conversation, and thus improves your own ability to talk your way to success.

Well, if you are going to devote much of your time to *listening* (as you should), when can you practice *talking* fluently (as you also should)? Of course, you should take an active part in every conversation—brief, but active. That's some practice, but not enough. The best way to learn to speak fluently is to over-do it. Since you can't do that with others without becoming a bore, you'll have to do it alone. Here's how:

Practice talking continuously—aloud—to yourself. Pretend that you are a radio announcer and that you have to "fill" a half-hour by ad libbing (talking spontaneously) without any "silent spaces". If you are alone at home, start by walking from room to room describing what you see. Speak in normal conversational tones. Talk continuously. Describe the furniture . . . where and when you got it . . . if it should be replaced or repaired. Describe the walls, ceiling, floor, everything in the room . . . what you think should be improved . . . and so on and on. Just keep talking . . . continuously . . . fluently.

Or, take a drive alone in your car—in the city or in the country. Pretend that you are a narrator, giving a travelogue of what you see as you drive along—and that you must give a continuous, interesting description of it in a conversational tone of voice. Describe the scenery . . . buildings . . . people . . . your impressions of them . . . and so on and on. If you drive to and from work alone every day, this is an excellent time to practice. To avoid the monotony of describing the same view every day, change routes frequently. Or just take a drive alone several or more times a week to practice talking fluently

If you have a friend who also wants to practice fluent talking, take your drives together. Alternate talking every ten minutes, vying to see who can give the most interesting and fluent performance of continuous scenic description.

Don't overlook the advantages of improving the *quality* of your speaking voice. Read several of the many excellent, self-help books on voice and speaking. Better still, take a speech course under a good instructor.

Finally, it is important to whom you talk. The more successful people you talk to, the more successful you, yourself, will be. While you should, for practice, for good-fellowship and for good-will, talk often to those of lesser or equal position, be sure to progressively devote more and more of your time to talking with top leaders in your company, in your civic and business community.

What can you talk about which will interest them? Remember those big, invisible signs they are wearing across their chests, reading: "I want to be IMPORTANT!" . . . I want to be ADMIRED!" . . . "I want to be APPRECIATED!" Talk to important people in those terms and *all* of them will *always* be interested in what you say.

Offer to *cooperate* with important people, especially in helping with their pet civic and charity projects. Your conversation—with your offer to help which it conveys—will always enable you to talk with ease with the most important people. Also it will lead to new contacts with other important people with whom to talk.

Offer profitable suggestions to the top executives of your company. But first try to be as sure as possible that your idea really will work. Let's face it. A top executive with long experience knows a lot more than a younger employee with much less experience (if that's what you are). That doesn't preclude your having better and profitable ideas. And you should suggest new ideas frequently. The point I want to make is: "*play it safe*" Always offer your suggestion in the form of a question. Say, "I've been wondering about (suggestion). What do you think about it?" . . . Or, "Have we considered the possibility that (suggestion)?" . . . Or, "What do you think would happen if (suggestion)?"

When you offer your suggestion in the form of an unassuming question and it is rejected, you can always say, "That is the conclusion I reached, too—but because of your greater experience, I wanted your opinion. Also, I thought you might be able to add some ideas that would make it practical." (That really gets the top executive *involved* in your suggestion and that's one of the secrets of success: *involvement with the top echelon!*) However, if your suggestion is accepted, *you* made it originally and *you* will get (or can modestly take) credit for it. Thus, by presenting your ideas in the form of questions, you benefit without risk) whether your ideas are accepted or not.

Having learned that you can *talk* your way to success, and having learned some of the many ways to do it, it is hoped that you will continue to learn more about this exciting and profitable success-method from the many helpful sources available.

Chapter 33

TALK! . . . A Way To Health

Probably this chapter should be more accurately titled: "TALK! . . . A Way To *Mental* and *Emotional* Health." Obviously, you cannot talk your way out of cancer or any primarily physical disease—and those cults and pseudo-curative professions are doing their believers a fatal disservice by encouraging faith in any other than the best possible treatment for each disease.

Thus having, I hope, warned against trying to apply a single cure to all illnesses, I want to discuss the amazing curative power of just talking. And, I want to start by explaining my use in the heading of this chapter of the word "health" instead of limiting it to "mental and emotional health".

First, to avoid repetition, let's consider "mental" and "emotional" as being mutually inclusive and use the word "mental" for both. (Many leading psychiatrists do.)

Next, let's understand that no disease is exclusively mental or physical, but a combination of varying proportions of both. The proportions may vary greatly, being mostly mental or mostly physical, but almost invariably both causes exist in some proportion.

Many people do not realize that *most* diseases have a primary *mental* cause, although the symptoms, and indeed the bodily damages, are demonstratively physical. These are called "psychosomatic" which the dictionary describes as: "bodily disorders induced by mental disturbances". It has long been known that more than half of all patients in doctors' offices and in hospitals are suffering from psychosomatic disorders (bodily illnesses, mentally caused). Progressively, more and more bodily disorders are diagnosed as being psychosomatic, even though the patient may not be so informed. Some extremists now declare that 90% of all illnesses have a primary *mental* cause.

A patient with a broken arm certainly feels that his accident was a physical happening as, of course, it was. What he may not realize is that behind the physical event was a mental desire to escape the responsibility of doing something which for some subconscious reason he did not want to do. People go blind, are partially or completely paralyzed, develop almost every imaginable illness (although some psychosomatic disorders are much more prevalent than others) as a means of escaping some repugnant situation, or in order to withdraw from some undesirable reality of life, or even as a form of self-punishment for a repressed sense of guilt.

In addition to the psychosomatic disorders with predominantly physical symptoms and often physical damage there is, of course, the entire spectrum of basically mental illnesses, ranging from simple self-consciousness to violent insanity. The situation has gotten completely out of hand. As Time Magazine stated some time ago: "If all the 15,000 (psychiatrists) in the United States, plus all the psychiatric social workers and all the psychologists trained as therapists, spent all their working hours with individual patients, they would still only be able to treat *one* in *ten* of the patients who need help for emotional ills."

I make no pretense of being qualified to provide a solution for so momentous a problem. I do want to suggest a simple—and highly successful—form of therapy which can be used to alleviate some mental and emotional stresses which often escalate into more serious disorders.

Dr. Karl Menninger, one of America's most famous psychiatrists, called it: "TALKING it out." More technically, psychiatrists call it: "Catharsis." The unprofessional simply calls it: "Getting it out of your system." To stay in the common vernacular, when something is "eating you", don't keep it to yourself—*talk* it out, get it out of your system. Don't worry and stew and fret *just by yourself* until you get "all steamed up" and then fail to "let off the steam"—because that's when you may "blow" in any one of a thousand disastrous ways!

Dr. Karl Menninger taught (in his excellent book, "The Vital Balance") that mental illness is not a lot of different illnesses, but actually consists of increasing stages of a basic mental disorder.

Certainly that is a greatly simplified and useful approach. It follows, since the first stage is the repression or some unwanted thought or act, resulting in a build-up of emotional tension and continued mental stress, that this increasingly dangerous condition can be relieved by a catharsis of whatever undesirable is being repressed—by getting it out of your system.

Specifically, the way to do this is to do just exactly what Dr. Menninger said, "TALK it out." Ever since Sigmund Freud developed the technique of psychoanalysis, the entire primary application of psychotherapy has been the patient's *talking out* his undesirable repressed thoughts.

The simple suggestions made here are no substitute for professional psychiatric treatment when a mental illness exists. Specifically, if whatever you are repressing is hidden so deep in your subconscious that it must be sought and exposed by psychoanalysis, you need the profesional services of a psychiatrist.

But, if you are fully aware of exactly what is bothering you and causing you emotional tension and mental stress, and if you want to "get it out of your system" —as you *must*—then you can do as Dr. Menninger advised and *talk it out.*

Once having reached the decision to *talk it out,* you have only to decide to whom to talk. That is very important, of course, and the sources are both numerous and adequate.

Naturally, the first choice is a psychiatrist, or a psychologist trained as a therapist. However, they not only are expensive, as such highly trained specialists must be, but their services are greatly in demand by the seriously mentally ill. Nevertheless, because of their vast knowledge, training and experience, they often can cure simple mental stresses in a few consultations.

Next, your regular doctor is an excellent choice. General M.D.'s now know a lot about psychotherapy and your own doctor has the added advantages of knowing a lot about you. Also, he will know whether you need more specialized assistance.

In all large cities, social service organizations provide trained personnel with whom you can *talk it out.*

The minister of your church has had a lot more experience in this field than you probably imagine. Large churches provide the services of a trained, full-time psychotherapist.

Your marriage partner may be an ideal person with whom you can *talk out* "what's eating you". His or her sympathetic understanding may be just what you need. I have always believed that, like charity, much psychotherapy should begin at home.

Or, *talk it out* with a trusted and sympathetic friend. But be sure to select the right person (not a gossip) and don't go around blabbing your intimate personal problems to everybody who will listen!

Whomever you *talk it out* with, get whatever is "eating you" out of your system entirely. Get rid of it! Be done with it! Then forget it!

That's one way to use TALK . . . as a way to health.

Here's another:

If you have a simple psychological problem

such as being self-conscious and embarrassed around peo ple and therefore not being a fluent conversationalist, you do not have to go to a psychoanalyst to learn the hidden psychological *cause* in order to be cured. It is not necessary to probe back into your childhood to learn that your mother spanked you undeservedly for your being "forward" when you were a child. That knowledge, even if correct, will not completely cure your self-consciousness. But *practicing conversing* with everybody at every opportunity about even the simplest subjects *will* cure your self-consciousness and make you a fluent conversationalist—whether your mother spanked you or not. (For more information on how to become a fluent conversationalist, re-read the previous Chapter 32: "TALK . . . A Way To Success".)

Participating frequently in interesting conversations, not only is good success training, but is good health therapy as well. It stimulates your interest in people, in ideas, and in life generally. It gets you involved. You participate. That's the key word: PARTICIPATE! . . . because participation is the sure antidote for withdrawal —and withdrawal is a mental illness which will progressively cause you more and more trouble, more and more unhappiness. Participation also is the sure antidote for mental depression which is, or can rapidly become, a serious mental illness.

So TALK is a means of staying healthy or becoming healthy. TALK, of course, will not cure everything—but it will cure many things and it will help in many ways to relieve the tensions and stresses of life, to help overcome fear, self-consciousness, withdrawal and depression. The list of the benefits of *talk* could go on and on—but I suggest you consider *talk* specifically in terms of any problem *you* may have. You'll be surprised how many times TALK will help!

Chapter 34

LISTEN!... A Way To Help

There are two sides to every coin.

In the two previous chapters, we have been looking at one side of a coin: "TALK". We found that you could *talk* your way to success (Chapter 32). And we found that, in many cases, you could *talk* your way to health (Chapter 33).

Now let's turn the coin over and examine the other side: "LISTEN". One should not consider *talking* without giving equal consideration to *listening*. They are two parts of a whole. Each is useless without the other.

Having learned the advantages of *talking*, let's discover the benefits of *listening*. Actually, listening is a way to help others. And, in helping others, you help yourself.

Remember what we said in other chapters about those big, invisible signs everyone wears across his chest . . . stating "I want to be IMPORTANT!" . . . "I want to be ADMIRED!" . . . "I want to be APPRECI-

ATED!" . . . remember that we said those invisible signs told us clearly how the other person wanted to be treated? Your success, your popularity, depends upon how well you heed those invisible signs, upon how you *help* others feel important, admired and appreciated.

One of the most effective ways to help others feel important, admired and appreciated is to *listen* to what *they* say with obvious admiration and appreciation, so that they know you consider what they say to be important. Thus, just by proper *listening,* you can use one of the most effective of all success-techniques: *help others get what they want.*

Remember, too, that you do not learn by talking—you only learn by listening. That's why you should listen a lot more than you talk.

If you listen with the proper attitude and if you listen to the right people—you can virtually *listen your way to success!*

But listening is more than that. *Listening is a way to help others* in other ways than to make them feel important, admired and appreciated, as just discussed. Psychiatrists agree that nobody is perfectly adjusted—mentally and emotionally—all of the time (if, in fact, *any* of the time!) Mental disorder is merely a matter of degree, with most of us fortunately being in Dr. Menninger's "First Stage" which consists primarily of the tensions and stresses, the disturbed feelings, occasional anxieties and mental depressions of normal life.

Relief from these pressures can be obtained principally by "*talking* them out" (as described in the preceding Chapter 33: "TALK . . . A Way To Health"). To "*talk* them out" a disturbed person needs a *listener* who is sympathetic, understanding and, hopefully, helpful.

Each of us needs to *talk* and to *listen* in order to relieve the tensions and pressures of daily living.

Probably the most frequent and vehement complaint of our time is that others will not *listen*.

Minority groups rage and riot because authorities will not *listen* (and therefore cannot be expected to respond) to their grievances and demands.

Students stage demonstrations to try to get the "Establishment", first to *listen* to their protests and dissent, and then to respond to their demands for change.

One of the principal complaints of youth is that their elders will not *listen* to their imaginative ideas. The elders reply that youth will not *listen* to the wisdom of more mature experience.

Example could follow example, but the need is already clear: *All of us must listen to each other.* Only by *listening*, can we fully understand, and, only if we fully understand *each other*, can we properly respond with *mutual* respect and earnest cooperation.

Chapter 35

When It Gets Darkest...

One of the world's greatest historians, having devoted a lifetime to studying and recording history from the beginning of civilization, was asked: "What was the most important thing you learned in your life's study of all significant historical events?"

He promptly replied, "When it gets darkest, the stars come out."

I consider that to be one of the most helpful and inspiring statements of all time! I hope you will remember it always, as I have. It will be a deep source of strength in your own dark hours. "When it gets darkest, the stars come out."

The proof is so voluminous, it is presumptuous for me to even begin to list examples. Yet I cannot leave it here. I cannot resist citing how, in the lives of three of the greatest men in history, it got darker than most people realize—and how, by some unexplained miracle, the stars came out.

John Stuart Mill, who later was to become the great English philosopher and economist, suffered a severe attack of mental illness, in 1826, when he was twenty years old. Szasz wrote that Mill was so overwhelmed by the most severe mental and emotional depression that he sank to the very depths of despair and was "suicidal" for many months. This was in 1826 when methods of curing such serious mental illness were not yet discovered. But . . . when it became darkest for John Stuart Mill . . . the stars came out. He completely reorganized his own personality, rapidly developed one of the greatest and most logical of minds, and became one of the greatest philosophers and economists of his time.

"When it gets darkest, the stars come out."

One of the greatest thinkers of all time was William James, the famed philosophical psychologist of Harvard. He was physically frail in his youth, developed severe psychosomatic symptoms affecting his eyes and stomach by the time he was twenty-three. Two years later he had to drop his studies entirely and go to Europe for many treatments. However, his mental-emotional disorders worsened and he suffered such extreme mental depression that he often contemplated suicide. Then . . . when it got darkest for William James . . . the stars came out. He completely overcame and transcended his physical and mental illness to become one of the greatest thinkers in history, a giant in philosophy and psychology, a famed writer, the most distinguished teacher at Harvard, whose wisdom has provided guidance and inspiration for so many of us through the years.

"When it gets darkest, the stars come out."

Dr. Karl Menninger, world-famous psychiatrist, records in his excellent book, "The Vital Balance", that Abraham Lincoln had, not one, but several, attacks of severe mental illness. Lincoln's own law partner described him as a "hopeless victim of melancholy" (one of the most serious of mental disorders). Indeed, Lincoln's future wife's relatives considered him "insane" and he reinforced their beliefs when, on his wedding day, after all preparations were made and the rest of the wedding party was waiting, he did not appear. Finally, after a search, he was found in his room in deep dejection, obsessed with ideas of unworthiness, hopelessness and guilt.

Dale Carnegie, who spent three years doing research on Lincoln's life and writing Lincoln's biography, wrote that Lincoln became dangerously ill in body and mind, and sank into a deep and terrible spell of melancholy, mumbling incoherent sentences and threatening suicide. He even wrote a poem about suicide and had it published in one of the Springfield papers. His friends took his knife away from him to keep him from killing himself.

Yet . . . when it was darkest for Abraham Lincoln . . . in some mysterious way (perhaps because there is a Purpose) . . . the stars came out.

You can see those stars now . . . stars on a field of blue in the flag of the United States of America . . . "One nation, indivisible, with liberty and justice for all."

In Springfield, Illinois, Lincoln's old home is preserved as a national shrine. And, because they lived nearby, a mother with her little girl, often passed it on their daily walks. As they passed Lincoln's home, the mother told her little girl about the greatness of Lincoln's presidential years and how much his life bestowed upon this nation.

Then, instead of passing Lincoln's home in daylight, the mother and her little girl happened to pass by one night. As was proper for a national shrine, the lights were aglow in every room. The little girl cried excitedly, "Look, Mother, look! Mr. Lincoln left the lights on!"

Yes, little girl, Mr. Lincoln did, indeed, leave the lights on! He left the lights on all over the world—to light our way toward freedom and equality and brotherhood for all men . . . everywhere!

Lincoln's life fulfilled the promise of history—when it got darkest, the stars came out.

Chapter 36

Do The Thing And You Will Have The Power

Fortunately, I learned one of the most useful facts of life at an early age. It is one of the great teachings of Emerson and I send him a mental message of thanks every morning when I wake up.

What I learned, as a very young man, was this:

"DO the thing and you will have the power!"

That one simple, yet almost-incredible, statement has enabled me: (1) To try; and (2) to actually accomplish things—more than any other statement I have ever heard.

If I had not believed, deeply *believed*, that just by the act of *doing*—somehow, from somewhere, I would be given the *power to do it*—I would not have attempted, much less accomplished, half of what I have done (the difficult, rewarding half).

How can this be possible, that the act of *doing* something generates the *power* to do it?

One answer comes from the psychologists. The most conservative psychologists say that a person never uses more than *half* of his actual capability. Others say that we are operating only at *one-tenth* of our capacity. Thus, depending on which psychologist is right, the very *least* you can accomplish is *twice* as much, and it may amount to *ten times* as much. So, since everybody normally operates at only a fraction of his potential, each of us can accomplish much more just by *trying* . . . just by *doing*.

DO the thing and you will have the power!

Henry Ford, who must have made some sort of record for doing things, put it simply, "Whether you *believe* you can *do* a thing or *not*—you are right."

Perhaps that's an over-simplification of a very profound fact of life. Nevertheless, there is a great reservoir of power ready to be used by anyone who begins to *do* something. *Do* the thing and you will have the power.

Maybe the ego calls on the super ego, which in turn draws the necessary power from an omnipotent ultra ego.

Or to state it in other terms, your conscious mind draws upon your subconscious mind, which, properly used, has at its disposal the unlimited power of the universal mind, which theologians call the God-Mind, or simply, God. Whatever the terminology, the *fact* is that there is an unlimited *supply* of power, and as you *do* the thing, you will have the power to accomplish it.

Thomas Edison believed that the power of his ideas came from "space". In the late years of his idea-filled life, Thomas Edison said, "Ideas come from space. This may seem astonishing and impossible to believe, but it is true. Ideas come from out of space." Edison should have known, because he had more ideas than any man who ever lived.

And if ideas come from "space", there is reason to believe that the power you need will come from "space", too. Certainly, whatever power—no matter how much power—you need to accomplish what you determinedly set out to do, *will be furnished you* from "somewhere". We have not evolved sufficiently to know all the answers. As a philosopher said, "Man's knowledge may be compared to a potato bug in a sack of potatoes in the hold of a great ship—wondering what makes the ship go".

But, because we do not know the *source* of our almost unlimited power for accomplishment, does not prevent our using the *fact* that such power does exist and is readily available for our use to achieve our goals.

So do not hesitate to strive for your goal. Start now—with the sure knowledge that whatever man can conceive and believe, man can achieve. Start now—without hesitation or fear, because the power to do, comes with the doing, and as ***you do the thing, you will have the power!***

Chapter 37

LAUGH... Your Way Through Life

You meet them everywhere—the Hypersensitive Ones! They find in every personal comment, a hidden insult . . . in every helpful suggestion, a subtle criticism . . . in every conversation, a challenge to debate.

These self-centered individuals find the most minor duties to be painful burdens, the imaginary weight of which only can be alleviated by overt recognition and bountiful praise. Routine activities become magnified projects. Necessary work is a hated, disagreeable thing to be endured. Complex plans are overwhelming and are resisted with undeserved panic.

The Hypersensitive Ones—their tender feelings are always being hurt and they respond with bitter sarcasm, unreasonable hostility or pained silence, which wins for them the questionable consideration and deference best described by that apt old-fashioned saying: "walking on eggs".

They are more to be pitied than condemned, because they suffer much more than do their understandably annoyed but nevertheless sympathetic companions.

The Hypersensitive Ones—why must they suffer so much unhappiness? Let's ask a famous psychologist, Dr. Maxwell Maltz.

Dr. Maltz says that the reason is self-pity. Then he describes their condition as follows: "The frustrated person compensates for self-pity by excessive smoking, excessive drinking, compulsive overwork (or imagined overwork), or withdrawal by escapism through radio, television or aimless reading—or turns upon other persons by exhibiting rudeness, irritability, nagging or fault-finding, stimulated by hypersensitivity.

You will meet many such people with exactly those syndromes (or most of them) in business, in school, among your associates, almost everywhere you go. (You might even try checking each symptom listed by Dr. Maltz to see if it applies to you!)

What do all these hypersensitive people have in common—EXCEPT the foregoing symptoms?

They seldom, if ever, laugh!

If hypersensitive people would only learn to laugh their way through life, they would be released from their self-centered unhappiness into a new, relaxed, joyful world of happiness and laughter.

Of course, there are times when laughter is out of place. I am not suggesting that you laugh in the presence of someone's sadness or at any time when laughter would be inappropriate. But you will find that such times, inevitable as they are, are proportionately few.

Nor am I suggesting that you boom through life with a Santa Claus "Ho! . . . Ho!! . . . Ho!!!" I am suggesting *quiet laughter*. Take an amused attitude toward yourself, your problems and difficulties, the situations and people causing them, and, especially, life itself. Laugh! And, if it is inappropriate to laugh heartily and openly—then laugh quietly . . . but *laugh*! It is the relaxed attitude of laughter—not the amount of noise you make—that determines your response toward your daily experiences.

What is *quiet laughter*? How can you do it? In two ways: First, do as recommended in Chapter 25: smile with your eyes. Then, say quietly to yourself, "Ha! . . . Ha!! . . . Ha!!!" Sound silly? Well, it isn't silly. It will mean making laughter, *quiet laughter*; or, when appropriate *rousing laughter,* a relaxing and joyful substitute for a tension-filled, hypersensitive, self-centered, unhappy life!

Remember, you can't be hypersensitive, self-centered and engulfed in self-pity while you *laugh* at yourself! So don't take yourself so seriously. There are so many things over which you must either cry or curse or laugh. Choose to laugh! *Laughter is your declaration of superiority over whatever befalls you!*

Against the assault of laughter, nothing can stand. Neither fear, nor worry, nor gloom, nor depression, nor resentment, nor hate, nor self-consciousness, nor hypersensitivity, nor self-pity can co-exist with laughter.

"He who has the courage to laugh, is master of the world nearly as much as he who is prepared to die."

Do you have an enemy? Then, if you have the courage (and the ability to defend yourself), *laugh* at him! There is nothing which so completely demoralizes an adversary more than being laughed at.

The only way to accept an insult is to laugh at it. (If you can't laugh at it, it probably is deserved.)

You can see from the foregoing that laughter is a *weapon*. A sure effective weapon. So *never* use the weapon of laughter by laughing *at* a friend. Only laugh *with* others, to *join with* them, to add your laughter to theirs. Only laugh *at* your enemies (knowing that they will then *remain* your enemies).

But mostly use your *weapon* of laughter to demolish your own undesirable personality traits: fear, anxiety, gloom, self-pity, resentment, hypersensitivity and all the raggle-taggle mob of disagreeable thoughts waiting to move into your mind the first time there is a vacancy. So keep those mental vacancies filled with laughter. Whenever your mind is not occupied with happy, positive, creative thoughts, fill it with quiet laughter—smile with your eyes (and with your entire face, when appropriate) and say over and over again quietly to yourself . . . "Ha! . . . Ha!! . . . Ha!!!" You (and everybody you know) will be amazed—and delighted—at the magic transformation of your personality when you begin to live with *laughter!*

It won't be magic, really. It will be simply that you have learned to use the delightfully devastating power of laughter so that you no longer take yourself too seriously.

Chapter 38

It's Right To Do It Wrong!

Psychologists have discovered an amazingly successful technique for eliminating undesirable habits—perhaps not all undesirable habits but, certainly, many of them.

We humans are largely creatures of habits, mostly desirable and, indeed, necessary habits. If we had to think consciously about everything we do, we would surely go mad. In fact, the more routine activities which we can assign to habit, the more we can free our time for conscious thought and action. A desirable or necessary habit, unconsciously and perfectly performed, is much better than a consciously directed action.

So most habits are desirable and we should try to shift more and more activities to our habit mechanism.

But some habits are undesirable, some are harmful, and some are extremely dangerous. Obviously these habits should be eliminated. Ridding yourself of bad habits is often exceedingly difficult. As the old Spanish proverb says, "Habits begin as cobwebs and end as cables." When they get to the "cable" stage, habits are not easily broken.

Because of the importance of habits—their formation, durability and elimination—psychologists have devoted much study and many experiments to them. It has been discovered that one of the easiest, surest and best methods of eliminating a bad habit is what is called: "Negative Practice."

"Negative Practice" has become such a valuable technique in personality improvement that it deserves a place in this book, and we shall devote the next few minutes to a brief study of it.

Since we are going to apply the technique of "Negative Practice" to the elimination of bad habits, let's see how bad habits get formed in the first place.

(1) A habit starts by being a conscious activity. You are fully aware that you are doing what you are doing, and whether you do it or not is a matter of your conscious control.

(2) Then, by repetition, the habit activity is directed less and less by your conscious, deliberate control and more and more, it is assigned to your unconscious (or subconscious) direction.

(3) Finally, you have no conscious control of the habit at all. It becomes a sort of conditioned reflex. When certain conditions exist, the now-unconscious habit is activated. The habit-action takes place whether you will it or not. In fact, the more will power you attempt to use

to stop it, the stronger you make the habit-impulse.

So how do you eliminate a bad habit? There really are many ways, but here we shall examine only one: "Negative Practice." Here's how to do it.

We have just outlined how a habit is formed. We stated that a habit starts as a conscious, deliberate activity and becomes, through repetition, an unconscious, impulsive response which is so ingrained that you cannot control it by conscious will power.

You eliminate the habit simply by *reversing the process* by which it was formed.

Specifically, you change it back from being an impulsive, unconscious, uncontrollable activity to a conscious, deliberate action which you can control and therefore eliminate at will.

This reversing procedure is accomplished by "Negative Practice". This means that you deliberately and consciously do—and *do excessively*—exactly what you want to eliminate doing habitually (impulsively, uncontrollably and unconsciously). When you *consciously, deliberately* and *excessively* repeat a habitual activity, you obviously are consciously and deliberately doing and *controlling* the action. That, of course, is exactly what you want, because then, since it is under your *conscious control*, you simply decide not to do it any more. And you *don't*.

If the habit does persist, you have not subjected it to enough "Negative Practice" to gain complete *conscious control* of it and so it is not subject to your will not to do it. So continue your "Negative Practice", remembering to do it *consciously, deliberately*, and *excessively*. Then apply *even more resolutely* your will not to do it. Sooner or later —usually sooner—you will eliminate the bad habit.

Let's consider a few of hundreds of possible examples:

Take stammering. There are many ways to cure stammering. All these cures are relatively easy, since physical defects are not usually involved at all. Stammering is caused by "tensing-up" to the point of immobilizing or "blocking" the normal, but highly complex, speech apparatus. The basic cause is self-consciousness and fear of repeating the embarrassing experience of stammering which by repetition has become an uncontrolled speech habit and a "conditioned response" to speaking to others. The direct cause is the blocking of the normal sequences of the speech impulse.

Many speech clinics use "Negative Practice" to cure stammering. In these speech clinics, the stammerer is required to deliberately and consciously stammer each and every word he speaks or reads. He actually practices stammering! He deliberately and consciously causes vocal blockage of every syllable of every word. He must always be acutely conscious that he is *deliberately forcing* himself to speak improperly—to stammer— and that *he* is controlling and directing this *wrong* method.

When he is fully aware that he is in complete, deliberate control of his stammering and that he is *consciously forcing* the vocal-blockage cause of his stammering —then he can *consciously stop* it! From then on it is simply a matter of learning the proper use of the voice in speaking and in overcoming self-consciousness in talking to others, both of which are easily accomplished by training and especially practice, so we won't attempt to detail the procedure to its final happy conclusion.

The point we want to make is that to eliminate a subconscious, uncontrollable habit, one first must get *conscious* control of it. This is done by "Negative Practice" —deliberately and consciously repeating the habit until it ceases to be subconscious and becomes a *consciously executed* action, which you therefore can *consciously stop.*

This principle of "Negative Practice" can be used to eliminate almost all habits. For example:

Fingernail biting can be eliminated by consciously and deliberately biting your fingernails for a half-hour at a time, always emphasizing that you are *deliberately forcing* yourself to do this silly thing. When this has been repeated sufficiently to become fully and embarrassingly *conscious,* you not only will be able to stop, but fingernail biting will have become so repulsive to you that even the thought of it will be revolting.

"Negative Practice" can be used to eliminate facial tics, teeth clicking, joint-popping, and all sorts of minor nervous habits. It will eliminate the involuntary repeating of errors in typing or writing certain words. It will eliminate bad habits you may have developed in golf, bowling or other sports, thus enabling you to greatly improve your style and form.

One use of "Negative Practice" by which all of us can benefit is the relief from involuntary tension in various parts of our bodies. Many people unconsciously clench their fists. This not only produces tension in them but it makes an unfavorable personality impression on others. This involuntary habit can quickly be cured and beneficial relaxation restored by the "Negative Practice" of consciously and deliberately clenching one's fists repeatedly, and then consciously opening and relaxing the hands. This same conscious "Negative Practice" can be used to eliminate unconscious muscular tension in all parts of the body. It is the most recommended and practiced form of relaxation therapy.

One note of warning. "Negative Practice" should NOT be used to eliminate habits where deliberate excess would be dangerous—such as drug addiction and alcoholism.

Otherwise, start now to eliminate any undesirable habits by the simple use of the proven psychological technique of "Negative Practice". The results are so fast and sure that it will be an enjoyable and rewarding experience!

Chapter 39

Walk Toward Danger

When I was a very young man, just starting out in business—without education, without money, without influential connections, without any of the alleged requisites for a successful career—I was fortunate in getting a little book: "Tips On Leadership" by Herbert N. Casson, whom B. C. Forbes called "the ablest writer on business and business men in the whole of Britain". Herbert Casson wrote equally well about American business and business men.

One of the many helpful principles I learned from Herbert Casson in his little book, "Tips On Leadership", was to WALK TOWARD DANGER. That precept has profoundly influenced my life.

I would rather live by those three words—WALK TOWARD DANGER—than have a college education. I also would like to have a college education, but many college graduates will never be leaders, even though they may be successful by other standards. *Nobody*, with or without a college education, can long be a leader unless he instinctively *walks toward danger* and naturally stands between his associates, his employees, or his followers—and *danger.*

The qualities of leadership are clearly shown in animal life. At the first sign of danger, the leader of the herd steps out of the crowd, stands apart from the others—and *walks toward the danger.* Always! Or he will not continue to be the leader.

That same thing is true in business, in politics, in civic affairs. A leader must do more than give directions and issue orders. He must protect those whom he leads. In times of danger, he must step out from the crowd. He must meet the challenge head-on—personally. He must *walk toward danger.* He must place himself between the danger and his followers. The first time he hesitates, the first time he falters—he will no longer be the leader. His followers will turn aside and follow another leader.

So you see, the risks of leadership are very great. Being a leader is no job for the timid. It requires more than brains and personality. Leadership requires courage—a special kind of instinctive courage. Leadership requires the kind of courage which is automatic. You do not ponder the pros and cons. You do not evaluate the risk. You do not count the personal cost. You instinctively step out from the crowd; you put yourself between the danger and those you lead. And . . .

WALK TOWARD DANGER!

Chapter 40

Grapple!

It has always been so, and the big word in problem-solving today is "GRAPPLE".

This word "*grapple*" is the principal admonishment to all who have problems (and who doesn't?). It is used by psychiatrists, psychologists, personal counselors and all who would give advice on problem-solving.

When any one word—and the action it stands for—is so highly and unanimously recommended, it clearly deserves our thoughtful consideration—and "*grapple*" shall receive it now.

Since grappling is the effective solution to problems, let's first look at the part which problems have in the lives of all of us. Not only do all of us have problems, but we seem to receive a regular daily quota of problems. They fall upon us much as the grains of sand drop through an hour-glass. And sometimes it seems with as much regularity. This continuous regularity with which problems come into our lives, is really good for us, although it may not seem so at the time.

Life without risks and obstacles and problems would not be worth getting out of bed for.

Happiness is not the absence of problems and difficulties. Happiness is successfully solving problems and effectively overcoming difficulties.

It requires just as much energy to try to escape from a problem as it does to *grapple* with it and conquer it. Try to escape, and your problem will follow you everywhere. *Grapple* with it and solve it, then it is gone forever.

Since new problems will always continue to come your way with a sort of continuous regularity, it is obvious that you must solve and dispose of them with equal regularity—or they will accumulate and eventually overwhelm you.

There are many broken men and women in this world, and almost every one has been broken in spirit, mind and body by the overwhelming burden of accumulated, unsolved problems.

Most mental and emotional illnesses can be traced in full or in part to the subjects' having become so overwhelmed by the continuing accumulation of unsolved problems that they were no longer able to cope with them and tried to escape through some form of mental maladjustment.

The same is true of much physical illness. Since 50% to 90% of all physical illness is psychosomatic (depending upon which psychiatrist's estimate you accept), most physical illness, too, can be traced back to the accumulating burdens of unsolved problems.

The only preventive is to solve your problems as they arise, so that unsolved problems will not accumulate. Obvious. But how?

That's where *grappling* comes in. Here is the advice of leading psychiatrists, psychologists and problem-solving counselors: To the extent that a person directly confronts the realities of a problem and actively *grapples* with it, he emerges stronger. To the extent that a person tries to ignore or escape from the realities of a crisis, large or small, he begins a worsening pattern of adjustment to life.

So by facing each problem directly, then plunging wholeheartedly into its very center and actively *grappling* realistically with it, you almost always will produce an adequate solution and you will emerge a stronger and more capable person.

Note that I said "adequate solution". That is an extremely important phase of problem-solving. Some people drive themselves and their associates to distraction by being perfectionists. They will accept nothing less than perfection. They insist on finding the "one best solution" to every problem. And thus they cannot reach decisions quickly and dispose of problems rapidly and with finality. They are forever reconsidering and re-examining. Meanwhile, other problems continue to come and to accumulate.

In this connection, efficiency experts (who know that *time* is an important element in efficiency) give this advice:

In the first place, there seldom is exclusively "*one* best solution" to most problems. There are often a number of "equally good solutions", any of which would be adequate, considering the expediency of quick decision. And an adequate solution, as the description implies, is *adequate*—and that's enough.

Besides, a second-best solution quickly decided and promptly put into effect is more efficient than a better solution which requires so much time in the making that a multitude of other problems accumulate.

So we see that we must not only *grapple* with our problems, but we must grapple with them immediately and reach an adequate solution promptly.

Problems will not go away because you ignore them. Problems cannot be out-distanced when you try to flee from them. You cannot escape them. You must face each problem in turn, plunge whole-heartedly into its center and *grapple* with it so actively that you reach an adequate solution—then put it decisively out of your life.

When I say "*grapple actively*", I mean really give it everything you've got! Be like the world-famous artist who was asked what he mixed with his red paints to solve the problem of producing a red which was so intense that he was acclaimed the foremost painter of his time. What did he mix with his red paints? He didn't even bother to look up from his work; he just quietly replied, "Blood".

GRAPPLE with your problems so aggressively that you put your *blood* into your *grappling!*

Life pays its highest rewards in fame and fortune to the problem-solvers!

The world is filling up with people, and this circumstance, alone, is a problem which threatens to overwhelm us. Then that problem is compounded by the fact that the multiplying multitudes have been misled to believe that griping is more productive than grappling. So they disrupt and destroy, thus creating more problems, including becoming problems, themselves.

We don't need any more problem-makers. We need problem-solvers, not the ivory-tower type, but the *grappling* type.

If you are a problem-solver, with the guts to *grapple* . . . the line forms at the cashier's window.

You can name your own price.

Chapter 41

DANGER! Do Not Threaten!

Perhaps, never before, has there been such imminent danger to so many people who do not even seem to realize that it is *they* who are causing this danger to *themselves*!

While this danger often is manifested in less vehement forms than physical violence, it is the violence of property destruction, personal injury and death, with which this chapter primarily will deal.

It is hoped that, by understanding the cause, at least the more intelligent activists will not deliberately bring this violence upon themselves and, directly or indirectly, upon others.

So that I shall not be accused of over-reacting to ominously increasing violence, let me assure you that the following psychological fact has been repeatedly demonstrated and verified thoroughout the entire history of mankind.

Let us simplify our analysis so that there can be no misunderstanding, and examine the one basic cause of this danger:

Danger is incurred by threatening others.

Let us get it clear—because this may be (already has been!) a matter of life and death. *Those who seek power by inflicting fear through threats are the ones in the greatest danger.*

The person who is threatened *may* be in danger; the person who makes the threat *is* in danger.

When one individual threatens another, the person who *makes* the threat instantly incurs the resentment, anger and hatred of the person threatened. And is in grave danger!

The purpose of a threat is to instill fear. But it does more than create fear and its accompanying insecurity; it instills anger and hate. If anger and hate cannot be vented by instant violence, they are suppressed, and seep into the subconscious which, in its hidden ways, seeks a means of eliminating the fear; therefore, the constant danger to the one *who made the threat* which caused the fear.

One of the most dangerous acts in which one can indulge, is to threaten another. And let us emphasize again, the greatest danger is to the person who *makes* the threat. The person who is threatened, usually has opportunity to prepare, and to choose the time, place and method of acting to halt the implementation of the threat. And, to retaliate.

To threaten another, is to set a time-bomb inside yourself, using a clock without hands or markings, and so never know when it will explode and destroy you.

Yet this kind of dangerous brinkmanship has become a reckless way of attempting intimidation. Almost every day's newspapers, television and radio news programs carry speeches which somewhere contain threats, direct or implied, against individuals, groups, races, classes, laws, governments, institutions, authorities—or whatever is the current threat-target of the activists, militants, disrupters, rioters, revolutionaries or anarchists in our midst.

These threats are made with foolhardy abandon which indicates a lack of knowledge of the danger to the one who, himself, is making the threat! Incredible as it seems, people think they can threaten others with impunity. *They cannot!*

The danger to the person *making* a threat is that a threat instills the fear of *loss* to someone or to many. It is a basic fact that while most people will *work for gain,* they will *fight to avoid loss.* Some may not choose to fight openly; some may not be able to fight immediately; but *every* person who is threatened by *loss* will re-act in some hostile manner and sooner or later will retaliate against the person (group, race, etc.) who threatened him.

The people who get their exhilaration of power through real or implied threats for the purpose of instilling fear in others, are placing *themselves* in grave danger. It is *they* who should be afraid, because as Seneca wrote in the days of the great Roman Empire, *"He must necessarily fear many, whom many fear.*" (That statement referred to Julius Caesar.)

People who make threats are not always in danger of assassination, although that sometimes is the case. More often, they are subject to injury. But much more often, they simply are rated "*undesirable and unacceptable*" as future employees, neighbors; and by the "Establishment" which they so vocally confronted and which they suddenly discover confronts them.

College graduates are finding it more difficult to get jobs. This is especially true of graduates of "trouble schools." (Business is noted for detailed record-keeping!) It may have been great fun—or even noble—to chase job-recruiters off the campus, but business personnel managers have a remarkable communication system, and data processing has a long memory.

Politicians, who become pawns of a vocal minority, will find that a minority (no matter how vocal and how dedicated) is still a minority in the voting booths.

Yet the threats continue; the threats multiply; the threats escalate in their radical demands. Clenched fists are raised as symbols of anarchy. But each threat assures subsequent retaliation. The day of accounting will come.

And those who seek power by instilling fear through threats are, *themselves*, in the greatest danger. It is the lesson of history.

It may not be too late to learn.

Chapter 42

"I Direct Your Attention To . . ."

It is a cliché often used by public speakers: "I direct your attention to . . ." Nevertheless, the directing of close attention is essential to the success of anyone attempting self-improvement.

The ability to direct your attention—to concentrate it—will almost, in itself, guarantee your success.

First, looking at it negatively, the failure to control the direction of your attention is the cause of many avoidable troubles.

From the irritated remark, "You're not paying attention to a single word I say"—to the fatal highway accident, inattention is as deadly to popularity as it is to driving.

In view of the fact that the human mind, acting subconsciously, does so many vital things with perfection without any conscious attention at all, it is perplexing that in many activities this is not the case, and controlled conscious attention is required.

Although the subconscious is the "storehouse of memory," we do not normally learn by subconscious exposure, but by conscious concentration. Often I have "read" several pages of a book while my thoughts drifted elsewhere, later to realize that I could not recall anything whatever of what I had just "read".

All memory courses are based on intense, conscious concentration of attention.

And although the driving of your automobile is largely subconscious, you must keep your conscious attention watching for sudden, unexpected hazards if you are to avoid them. Most automobile accidents are the result of not consciously concentrating on "defensive driving." You must keep your attention on the inattention of other drivers.

The "absent-minded" person simply is the victim of not paying conscious attention.

Much has been written about the vast power and amazing ability of the subconscious mind. (Indeed, I, too, have written much about it.) And while the subconscious mind does independently perform such amazing feats as operating our bodily functions (heartbeat, breathing, and all the rest) and through cybernetics may even guide our personal destinies, let us not overlook the necessary directing power of our conscious minds.

Our subconscious cannot reason. It can only perform, in its own wonderful way, the tasks assigned to it by our reasoning, conscious minds. So let us be ever conscious that our conscious minds are the directing force of our lives—for good or bad. Our conscious thinking makes it so.

And let us remember, too, in these days of hallucinatory drugs which block out the reasoning, conscious mind so that one can take a "trip" in his uninhibited subconscious, that the weird visions conjured up do not compare with the detailed beauty which can be enjoyed by focusing your conscious attention on the wonders of nature all around you—the simple beauty of a rose, the breathtaking view from a mountain top, the restless rolling of the deep, green ocean, the unrestrained joy of a happy child.

The penalties for not paying attention are so severe and the rewards of focusing concentrated attention are so great that I want to close this brief essay as I opened it—with the public speaker's cliché: "I want to direct your attention to . . . ATTENTION."

It just might make a big difference in your life.

Chapter 43

Are You Lonely?

There are many people who, by the nature of their lives, occupations or circumstances, spend considerable time alone.

This does not mean that they are lonely.

Being alone may—or may not—contribute to loneliness. As a matter of fact, people who are subject to the feeling of loneliness may experience its symptoms while being in a crowd. Remember the line in the old song, "I could be lonely out in a crowd"?

Feeling lonely is a neurosis which can intensify and escalate through various stages of annoyance, irritability, depression and finally end up being a full-fledged psychosis which psychiatrists call "monophobia".

Since, from its unpleasant early stages to the extreme morbidness of its monophobia stage, loneliness is so entirely undesirable—if you experience even its mildest forms, get rid of it!

Getting rid of loneliness not only is simple and permanent, but its elimination provides the double enjoyment of decreasing unhappiness and increasing happiness every easy step of the way.

The first and all-important step in eliminating loneliness is to recognize what it really is. And this may surprise you! Most people think of loneliness as "being alone" or "missing somebody". So they never get at the real cause, and therefore don't find a cure.

Psychiatrists say that loneliness is *not liking yourself!* It is not being able to get along with yourself when you are alone and your attention tends to center on *you* as you imagine yourself to be. Loneliness is not liking the quiet environment when you must confront yourself with yourself and decide what to do next with *you* . . . alone. It is not liking yourself even in a crowd and experiencing a feeling of withdrawal because of it until you feel apart from others and "alone in a crowd".

Let's face it. The person you're going to have to spend the most time with is you. All others, no matter how dear, how companionable, or how interesting, cannot be with you every minute or every hour or every day—and for various reasons, the time may come when they will not be with you at all.

Since you are going to spend all of the rest of your life with you, you might as well learn to like yourself. This does not mean be egotistical. (People are not nearly as egotistical to themselves as they appear to be when trying to impress others.) People, when they are alone, tend to evaluate themselves very much as they really *think* they are. That is why not liking yourself and therefore *especially* not liking being *alone* with yourself causes the mental and emotional discomfort known as loneliness.

That subconscious mind of yours starts digging up and parading before your conscious mind unpleasant thoughts involving you—and you don't like it. Psychiatrists have found that the hypersensitive, irritable, annoying, criticizing, nagging people who are quick to use those unpleasant qualities to hurt others, are the ones who turn those same qualities *inward* when they are alone. Perhaps they feel a sense of guilt. Anyway, they feel lonely.

We can state it more simply. If you get along well with others, you will get along equally well with yourself—and you will have eliminated the basic cause of loneliness.

But what to do when you are alone? One of the most rewarding things to do is *nothing!* Actually it is far from being nothing, but it does consist of almost total physical inactivity. This physical inactivity when you are alone enables you to engage in two of the most enjoyable and rewarding mental and spiritual activities:

(1) MEDITATION

(2) CONTEMPLATION

Let's consider the rewards of (1) MEDITATION. There comes a thunderous command: "Be *still*, and know that I am God!" And every religious leader, every philosopher, every thinker, every great and good man and woman has heeded those words, has gone off *alone* to a quiet place, has been *still* and meditated . . . and listened *spiritually*.

I don't need to make a case for it. I need only ask you to read their biographies. Any of them. All of them. Was Jesus lonesome when He spent forty days and forty nights—alone—in the wilderness? Was Thoreau lonesome during the years he spent—alone—at Walden Pond? One of the most fulfilling, rewarding experiences of life is to be *alone,* to be *still,* to listen *spiritually* . . . to *meditate.* I promise you won't feel lonesome.

Now let's consider the other physical inactivity in which you can engage mentally and spiritually when you are alone: (2) CONTEMPLATION. This is an art, the joys of which are indescribable. It is the art of thoughtful attention to almost anything until you "identify" with it —spiritually become a part of it. Contemplation can include everything from bird-watching to art appreciation, to just contemplating the sheer incredibility of the infinite detail of the "everyday" things you see outside the window, or inside the house.

The people who annoy me most are those dull blobs who sit in airplanes with their faces buried in magazines in the blasé attempt to give a sophisticated impression that this is "just another routine bus ride, all in the day's work." And now the airplane movie-watchers! Well, I happen to have flown on quite a few planes in various parts of the world, myself. And every plane trip is an exhilarating experience! There, hopefully, are clouds, always different, always changing. Always magnificent! And I am *in* them! In daylight, there is the panorama of the earth below, with its kaleidoscope of patterns made of crazy-quilt workings of man and nature. At night, from the window of a plane, I look down on jewels of light, some scattered, some bursting in massed splendor like exploding skyrockets. This is a fragment of the universe, and through contemplation, I am happily involved in it! Lonely? Amid all this!

If you will but look, you will find the opportunities for contemplation are as limitless as . . . well, as *every thing!* And the deep, satisfying spiritual joy of quiet contemplation is just as limitless. You cannot be lonely when you are absorbed in contemplating the vastest or the tiniest parts of this mysterious, magnificent universe.

Of course, you do not need an airplane or any form of travel to enjoy your world. If you cannot, or do not choose to leave your easy chair, the world will come to you through books, publications, radio and television. And not just the world as an ever-fascinating spectacle—but its interesting people of today and on back through history. You can examine their lives, their thoughts, their deeds. Again, you have readily available to you . . . contemplation unlimited. And a sure cure for loneliness—forever!

One of the recommended cures for loneliness is to "lose yourself in busy activity", be it vigorous work or active play, or some difficult puzzle or game which requires your full mental concentration. If you "lose yourself" simply as a means of escapism—of escaping from yourself temporarily—then this method of escape will soon come to an end, leaving you enervated physically, mentally, and emotionally, more subject to the symptoms of loneliness than when you began this grimly trying to "lose yourself". But if you use work, sports, play, concentration games, for the sheer fun of enjoying and expressing *yourself* in happy activity, then, of course, you have found a sure and exciting cure for loneliness.

Obviously, being with people you love, or like, or in whom you can find some interest, prevents or alleviates loneliness. I mention this situation last because some people place so much dependence on just being with others that they shrink from facing their own selves—alone—for any appreciable length of time. Yet you and I and all of us are going to spend the rest of our lives with our own selves. And, as I have pointed out earlier, all others, no matter how dear, how companionable, how interesting, cannot be with you every minute or every hour or every day—and, for various reasons, the time may come when they will not be with you at all.

So, look first to yourself and *like* yourself. If you cannot *accept* yourself, as you now are, then you're going to have to change yourself into the kind of person you can accept, like and get along with—alone. Because, if you cannot get along with yourself—alone—then all the escapism you can devise, will not prevent loneliness.

But, if you can enjoy being with *you,* you have a life-time companion who will be with you always, to seek out the unlimited miracles of a universe filled with things to see and do, or just to read about, to meditate upon, or to contemplate in the depths of your exploring spirit.

When you *like being with you*—you'll never be lonely.

Chapter 44

Find Out

The world belongs to those who find out.

Show me the person who can find out what the trouble is—and how to fix it—and I will guarantee that person's success in life, business, and the pursuit of happiness.

There is nothing more demoralizing to personal stability than a life full of question marks.

There are very few activities more satisfying and rewarding than finding the answers to questions, the solutions to problems.

We need people who can get things done. But even more, we need people who can find out what needs to be done and the best way to do it. The world is full of people who are doing something—and doing it wrong. The world is full of people who know all kinds of things—and what they know is wrong. They didn't find out.

It would be better if they did nothing, knew nothing. Then they could start with a clean slate. They could find out first, so that what they thought, said, and did, would be right. There is no advantage in being wrong—even if you're wrong first. It is much more profitable to take the time required—and be right later.

All governments are full of people busily doing wrong things, deciding on wrong policies, and expensively carrying them out in the wrong way, with the wrong results. Our own nation's history is a long record of how to do things wrong—not because we didn't try—but because we didn't find out.

Business makes a big project of doing things wrong. Maybe computers will help. But my experience with computers doesn't bear out that hopeful conclusion. When a computer makes a mistake it is so astronomical or so repetitive that a hundred people doing things wrong couldn't equal it. I have spent my life in business. I'm retired now, so I have plenty of time to look back on all the mistakes I made. I even have analyzed them. Sort of post-mortem. I have concluded that all the many mistakes I made could have been avoided simply by finding out.

Education is supposed to be devoted to finding out—and that's good. The trouble is that education doesn't start at the beginning. The ultimate purpose of education should be to enable you to succeed—and I define success as the attainment of your goal in life. To do this, education must *first* provide you with three fundamentals:

(1) INSPIRE you with real, believable facts which will convince you that you *can* and *will succeed.*

(2) MOTIVATE you first to find out what you need to know and what you need to do to assure your success—and then continue to motivate you, throughout your entire life, to do *whatever* your success requires.

(3) Teach you a simple SUCCESS FORMULA which you easily and always can use to achieve your goal in life.

That's not all there is to education, but it is the necessary beginning.

In government, in business, in education, and in everyday living, if you want to be great, if you want to be acclaimed, if you want to be rich—find out what the trouble is and find out how to fix it. You don't have to fix it personally. There are plenty of people to do the actual work. But the big rewards go to the person who FINDS OUT.

Chapter 45

Success Begins With Three

It is the unique plan of this book that each chapter shall be unrelated to preceding chapters. The purpose is to give you entirely different "Thoughts To Build On", and thus add variety to brevity.

However, in this chapter, I want to say a little more about one idea mentioned in the previous chapter. It has to do with education and the three things with which education must begin, if it is to guarantee your success in achieving your goal in life.

Most formal education today begins with an empty fuel tank. It has no motive power. It begins by loading you down with facts before it gives you an operating vehicle with which to use those facts to reach a goal —SUCCESS.

Obviously, in the early years of life, success cannot be defined in specialized terms of specific careers. So it will have to range from the initial concept of: "CAN

DO" to as far as available imagination can see. The degree will depend on the stage of development.

But that does not affect the premise that there are preliminary essentials which must precede every educational and training process:

First, you must be INSPIRED with real, believable facts which convince you that you *can* and *will succeed.* That is the ignition which ignites the fuel in the rocket to propel your guided missile to success. No ignition—and you stay on the ground. There are too many lives which are grounded because nobody provided the ignition of *inspiration.*

Next, you must be MOTIVATED to find out what you need to know and do in order to *assure* your success. Motivation converts inspiration into activity. But activity, no matter how nobly inspired, can be good or bad. It does no good to heroically mount your steed and then frantically ride off in the wrong direction. So your inspiration must be sufficiently motivated for you to be willing to pay the price of your success in terms of a *predetermined* goal. There must be a goal and it must be predetermined—otherwise you will be accumulating facts for which you will have no future use.

Whatever you want from life has a price tag. Not just in money. Money usually is involved, but that is unimportant, since anybody can get whatever amount of money he needs. It is the other things included in the price of success which you must be willing to pay—the personal sacrifices in time, effort, study, planning, finding out, going, doing. Formal education too often fails to provide sufficient directional motivation along with the facts.

Finally, there is a third essential which—together with inspiration and motivation—must precede every educational and training process.

You must be given a simple, easy SUCCESS FORMULA which you can use to achieve *whatever* you want in life. It is incredible that people do not understand the development and use of a success formula. I know of no college or university, high school or vocational school, which teaches a real, genuine, sure-fire success formula. Yet, together with inspiration and motivation, a success formula is one of the three fundamentals with which useful education and training must begin.

The government—at all levels: federal, state and local—is engaged in all sorts of educational and training programs to help the underprivileged become more successful. Yet, these government-financed programs which require billions of dollars of the taxpayer's money, do not start with providing the underprivileged with the three fundamentals they must have first before the education and training they receive can be meaningful and directional.

Make this simple test. Look at the pictures of the underprivileged on television or see them in real life as they live their aimless, hopeless, poverty-retarded existences. Then ask yourself these simple questions:

(1) Are the underprivileged INSPIRED with a positive belief that they *can* and *will succeed* in *earning* a full share of the abundance of our affluent society?

(2) Are the underprivileged MOTIVATED first to find out what they need to know and do to *earn* success and are they enthusiastically learning and doing those things right now?

(3) Do the underprivileged have an easy, simple, proven SUCCESS FORMULA which they *now* continuously use to guide them directly to success, to enable them to attain *whatever* they want?

(4) If the underprivileged are not now provided with these first three fundamental essentials of success, why aren't they? Whose fault is it? Why isn't this fault immediately corrected?

Chapter 46

When Personal Tragedy Comes

This is not a happy chapter to write—but it needs to be written in the hope that some day it will diminish heartbreak into heartache, then gently substitute the healing of an acceptance which asks not understanding.

Because into each life—sometime—personal tragedy will come, inevitably, as a part of life . . . and death.

There are explanations of this. Choose one if it helps. It is not our purpose here to examine explanations, but to seek relief.

Nor shall we morbidly list personal tragedies for they are sufficient unto themselves. We shall state simply that the personal tragedies of our lives are our losses of things or, more often, of persons, very dear and very much a part of us.

Then they are gone.

What shall we do? What *can* we do? What MUST we do?

Four things.

Other things, too, perhaps—but always these four, because just as personal tragedy is inevitable, these four steps to recovery are infallible.

Each of the four is spelled beginning with an "A", which makes them easy to remember when grief blurs our thoughts: A . . . A . . . A . . . A.

(1) ADMIT: First, you must ADMIT that the tragic loss *has* occurred. There may be temporary relief in numb disbelief. But the anesthesia of disbelief wears off in confrontation with fact and encourages withdrawal from reality in a vain attempt to sustain escape.

There is a mental danger in playing make-believe with tragedy. It is better (in fact, it is *necessary* if you are to maintain sanity) to face tragedy frankly, squarely, honestly. There is relief and strength in the courage to meet reality boldly and openly, to ADMIT that what is so, IS so.

Only when you have taken the first step, ADMIT, is it possible to obtain the merciful relief of the next step toward peace of mind and spirit:

(2) ACCEPT: By fully *admitting* your tragic loss, you open the way to what probably is the greatest and most rewarding of all mental, emotional and spiritual powers: ACCEPTANCE.

Acceptance of the inevitable is one of mankind's greatest achievements. In recognizing the human inability to control all circumstances, ACCEPTANCE gives man mastery over the *consequences* of those events he cannot control.

And so, with personal tragedy. Complete ACCEPTANCE of it—with humility and submission—quietly, but surely, gives you the mastery of survival and the inner resources to deal with whatever consequences may result.

No one is given a burden without, at the same time, being given the strength to bear it.

Willingness to ACCEPT the inevitable misfortunes of life transcends almost every other human power. It is useless to fight the inevitable—or to reject it, or curse it, or hate it. On an ancient cathedral in Holland is inscribed the eternal truth: *"It is so. It cannot be otherwise."*

We can deal with such finality only through ACCEPTANCE, as philosopher William James advises, "Be willing to have it *so*. ACCEPTANCE of what has happened is the first step to overcoming the consequences of any misfortune."

And, in the philosophy of Schopenhauer, "A good supply of resignation is of first importance in providing for the journey of life."

By ACCEPTANCE you attain a spiritual transition from sorrow to tranquility.

But what then?

If we (1) ADMIT and (2) ACCEPT, we achieve peace of mind. But then must we, like Buddha, lose ourselves in idle, serene contemplation?

Believing there is more to make of life than that, we move forward, taking Step Number Three—the third "A":

(3) ADAPT: The act of ADAPTING gives validity to *admitting* and *accepting*—it is the third dimension which imparts substance, otherwise there remains only a passive state of mind, helpful as that is, but nothing more.

It is the act of ADAPTING, the ego-involvement in making whatever changes are necessary to adjust completely to *all* of the circumstances of your misfortune, which excludes the imminent possibility of withdrawal. You must become willingly and totally involved in *whatever* adjustments are necessary, because withdrawal from reality soon becomes a severe mental illness.

Your ADAPTING must come from within. Your adjustment to the changed situations resulting from misfortune must be voluntary and without reservation. Your adjustment must be *total* . . . and it must be *yours*. It must bear the hallmark of *your* courage, *your* determination, *your* decision.

Thus, because *you*: (1) ADMIT, (2) ACCEPT, and (3) ADAPT . . . you attain a spiritual transition of indescribable magnitude.

What more can you do?

One more thing. One more "A", perhaps the easiest because it is made possible by your having completed the first three steps, but this final "A" will put you back into the mainstream of life:

(4) ACT: The ultimate achievement in dealing with the consequences of tragedy is to ACT at once, leaving the door which Fate forever closed, and ACTIVELY seeking the open door which Faith promises, "Seek

and ye shall find." For it is a Law of Life that when Fate closes one door, Faith opens another.

And what is beckoning to you beyond the Door of Faith? There is an ACTIVITY in which you can lose your SELF—in a cause of your own choosing, an activity which will occupy your thoughts and energies, and which is bigger than you and, therefore, bigger than any feeling of tragedy which may still possess you.

You must seek your *own* channel of ACTIVITY . . . find your *own* cause . . . and then put your entire SELF into it, leaving no part of YOU behind to relive, again and again, the regret, the remorse, the grief of a tragedy you cannot now undo. You must find the motivation to ACT—to WORK—physically and mentally, to help *others,* thus losing your in-growing SELF-consciousness of tragedy by replacing it with an out-going OTHERS-consciousness of helpfulness.

Hard physical and mental WORK (the more constructive and worthwhile, the better) will relieve and replace emotional tension, anxiety and grief, and will provide the healthful exhaustion which assures relaxing rest in the satisfying glow of accomplishment. The ACTIVITY you choose must be more than an occupation—it must be a dedication.

So the total: A + A + A + A: (1) ADMIT, (2) ACCEPT, (3) ADAPT, and (4) ACT . . . the infallible combination which, used in that order, will reveal the Door of Faith through which you can walk confidently into a new life . . . serene and assured—busy with the present, secure in the knowledge that you can accept and surmount such inevitable vicissitudes as the unpredictable future may bring.

Where is the source of such additional power as you may need to achieve these results?

The power is provided by the very act of your DOING, because it is a Law of Life that, if you act in faith, as you *do the thing*, you will *receive the power*.

Thus your capability to survive and then surmount personal tragedy finds its power-source in your consummate faith that you are a part of Infinity which, being total perfection, can harbor no problems—including *yours*—and so, with unlimited resources, absolves your problems when you have the wisdom and faith to release them.

Chapter 47

The Sympathy Seekers

This world does not have a very good reputation for treating its temporary occupants with tender loving care. So if you want to invoke sympathy, you will not lack opportunities.

But if we are to cope with our problems, we need less sympathy and more determination.

Annette Kellerman was lame and sickly. Did she want sympathy? No, she wanted a perfect body. With determination, exercise and professional treatment, she developed a perfect body. She was judged one of the world's most perfectly developed women. She also became the World Diving Champion.

Sandow started life as a sickly weakling. Now, the last thing Sandow wanted was sympathy. He wanted strength! He determinedly exercised until he developed one of the most perfect bodies in history and became the strongest man of his time.

Some years later, a lame, weak little boy named George Jowett decided that determination was more constructive than sympathy. He was right. Instead of feeling sorry for himself and wanting others to feel sorry for his lameness and weakness, he charged and re-charged his mind and body with determination. What happened? No miracle. Just the natural Law of Cause and Effect. It always works. In ten years, George Jowett became the world's strongest man.

Then there was poor, blind, deaf, mute Helen Keller. Did she want sympathy? No. She was determined to surmount her handicaps and to devote her life to helping others (who were not nearly so handicaped!). She became one of the most inspiring women of all time. And it is important to note that Helen Keller did not eliminate her physical handicaps—that was impossible. What Helen Keller did was to use determination to *surmount* her handicaps and achieve greatness *while* she was handicapped!

Modern medicine can eliminate most physical handicaps. Even then, determination is a great factor. Often the first attempt at a cure does not work. So people become sympathy-seekers instead of cure-seekers. As Edison did with his experiments, you have to have the determination to persist, sometimes through many failures, until finally a solution is found. One of the best therapies is to keep busy seeking a cure!

There are, of course, some physical handicaps like Helen Keller's blindness, deafness and muteness which cannot be completely cured. Then you, like Helen Keller, must not seek sympathy, but use determination, to *surmount* your handicap and achieve a happy, satisfying life *while* you are handicapped—*in spite* of your handicap—or, better still, *because* of your handicap.

Beethoven wrote his immortal symphonies when he was deaf.

Milton wrote *Paradise Lost* when he was blind.

Alexander Pope was so crippled that he hardly could move, yet he became one of the giants of English literature.

Julius Caesar was epileptic, yet he conquered the then-known world. When he felt an epileptic seizure coming on, he gave instructions for carrying on the battle while he was unconscious. When he regained consciousness, he calmly resumed command as though nothing had happened.

Franklin D. Roosevelt, crippled by infantile paralysis, became President.

In a prison cell, John Bunyan wrote *Pilgrim's Progress*, a book that is one of the epics of English literature.

Robert Louis Stephenson was never, even for one hour, free from pain and a hacking cough. He suffered from fever and tuberculosis. Yet he wrote *Treasure Island* and many exciting or humorous stories.

We could fill the rest of this book and many additional volumes just giving examples of the crippled, the sickly, the physically handicapped, who disdained sympathy and by sheer determination achieved the greater solace of surmounting their infirmities.

There are countless thousands who daily surmount their handicaps by accepting them and adapting to them. They seek no sympathy; they ask no privileged assistance. These people, whom we call "handicapped", go about their daily lives with acceptance, determination and ingenious adaptation which should make those of us, who are less handicapped, ashamed of our petty complaining and our pleas (or demands) for custodial care from some form of beneficent society.

There are those without arms, who operate automobiles and machinery with their feet.

There are those without legs, who move about with agility by using their arms, or with artificial limbs.

There are the blind, whose accomplishments are no less than miracles to those of us who have not been confronted with the challenge of continuous total darkness.

They are not sympathy-seekers. They have compensated for their handicaps by attaining a quality of character which many of the more fortunate of us should persistently seek.

Chapter 48

Externalize Yourself. Don't Exist!

This is a psychological technique which may eliminate self-consciousness, make you more popular than you ever dreamed possible, make you a master of the rewarding art of conversation, change your entire life for the better (which is an understatement).

In all fairness, I also should tell you that externalizing themselves may be difficult for most people at first. Not impossible. Just difficult—because it requires breaking a bad habit. And the resulting feeling is a little strange. But it's fantastically exciting!

What most of us do—and have done all our lives—is internalize ourselves. Which simply means we think about ourselves and we relate other people and events to ourselves, our families, friends and possessions. That's nothing of which we need be ashamed since it is an intinct with which we were born. It is our inheritance from prehistoric man who had to devote almost his full time to himself and the effect of his antagonistic environment on himself.

Now let's consider what would happen if we were to reverse the process and externalize ourselves. We would, insofar as possible, think of others and think in terms of their needs, desires, hopes, plans, interests and involvements with life.

We would, insofar as possible, "not exist" in our own minds. Only others would exist.

Well, what would happen?

Let's consider fear. Fear usually is anticipated danger to ourselves, our families, friends or possessions. When we stop thinking about ourselves, we immediately stop being afraid. Thus we eliminate fear and its related anxiety and worry.

For example, take the fear of meeting and talking to strangers. We are SELF-conscious and feel a sense of anxiety concerning a possible poor impression we may make and thus damage our SELF-image. But change SELF-consciousness to OTHERS-consciousness, eliminate the concern for your SELF-image and the conditions for fear for yourself vanish. You are poised, undisturbed, at ease, unafraid. Obviously, the impression you will make will be greatly improved.

Now, consider the result of externalizing yourself in your conversations. YOU "don't exist". Only OTHERS exist. So your conversation is entirely about them, their families, their interests, their successes, their aspirations. Would not this make you a much more interesting conversationalist to *them?* And since they naturally know more about themselves than you do, this would enable them to do most of the talking—an additional star in your conversation crown.

Example could follow example, but, for the sake of brevity, let's go for the jack-pot now and consider externalizing your entire attitude toward life. Don't think "inside" about you, your aches and irritations, your annoyances and troubles . . . but think "outside"—externalize your thinking—"don't exist" except as a force for helping others and making this a better world and a better life for as many others as you can.

Don't do this for appreciation or reward because, remember, YOU "don't exist". You will have become a part of a much bigger thing—something so much bigger that some call it . . . INFINITY.

Chapter 49

Infinity Has No Problems

So you have problems? Troubles? Fears, worries, anxieties?

Sure you do. But do you know why? It's because you are a human being and, like all the rest of us, just aren't big enough, powerful enough, intelligent enough, not to have problems, troubles, fears, worries and anxieties. And, unfortunately, neither you nor any of us can ever be that big, that powerful, that intelligent.

So, that's that. Or . . . is it?

Perhaps we can get some help. Where? Well, is there anything which does not have problems? Sure. Infinity has no problems. Everything works exactly, perfectly. Always does. Undoubtedly always has. Everything in the whole universe, from planets to electrons, works perfectly. No problems. Perfection. That's what Infinity is . . . perfection.

And, Infinity is something else. Infinity is EVERYTHING. That makes Infinity important—and *per-*

sonal—to YOU! Because EVERYTHING, which is Infinity, includes YOU.

That makes YOU a part of the Infinite which is so big, so powerful, so intelligent that it has no problems, no troubles, no fears, no worries. And, since you are a PART of the Infinite, you are a PARTNER of the Infinite.

There's help! More help than you'll ever need! The trouble with most people is that they never realize that such help is available to them, anytime, any place, anywhere. Suppose you were a partner of a billionaire—and never knew it. It would never do you any good. And that's just a trivial example compared to being a part of —a partner of—the Infinite.

If you want your partner to help you, you have to be constantly aware of your partnership. Assign all of your problems, troubles, fears and worries to Infinity, which having no problems, will dispose of yours with Infinite wisdom and power—thus continuing to have no problems.

People have difficulty dealing directly with anything so unlimited as Infinity. Naturally. So, many people personalize Infinity and, in this part of the world, they call Infinity . . . God.

Chapter 50

Life Is A Mirror

This is going to be a sort of trite chapter—because I (and others) have written about this truism often and in many ways. Yet it intrigues me so much that I must write about it once again.

I am deeply fascinated by the fact that each of our lives is the exact reflection of our own selves. Life is a mirror which always reflects what we think, how we feel, what we do and—especially—what we really are.

It is a sobering thought. It should cause one to pause in his day's moods to witness his reflection in the mirror of his life.

As we grow older the picture of our past is etched in the lines of our faces and illuminated, dimly or brightly, in the depths of our eyes. The old saying that others can "read us like a book" might better be expressed that they can "observe us like a picture"—and almost instantly judge us.

But, some say that appearances are misleading. And so they are—sometimes—if we judge by physical appearances only. Many people have been known to change their characters and personalities more rapidly than nature can change the outward physical manifestations of their new selves. So the novices in character and personality judgment often are misled, as novices usually are in every field.

Life, nonetheless, is an accurate mirror. But it is much more than the usual plate-glass mirror in which we see ourselves every day. The mirror of life shows not only our outer appearances, as we have created them, but, it reveals our inner selves—our characters, our mental depths and emotional stabilities, our personality traits and degrees of magnetism.

It is the sum total of our outer and inner selves which makes up our real reflections in life's mirror—which are more than visual reflections, but are auras which can be sensed as well as seen.

If this were only a matter of observing our real selves as we have created them, it would be merely an interesting and revealing phenomenon. But it is much more.

It is the creator of our destinies!

We not only become the sum total of everything we have thought, experienced and done in our past, but in so becoming, our natures determine our responses to events which constitute our lives.

It simply is a chain of causes and results. What we think, feel and do, causes us to be what we are. And what we are, causes the circumstances and events of our lives.

Do not be so naive as to delude yourself that your life is a happening of fate. It was caused—principally by you—and it is a mirror which accurately reflects what you now are.

If you don't like what you see in life's mirror—you can always change it. Simply by changing YOU.

Chapter 51

Inner Pace For Inner Peace

Those, who have thought deeply, have referred to inner pace in different ways:

" . . . like muffled drums are beating . . . "
" . . . your personal inner rhythm . . . "
" . . . your own private pace . . . "
" . . . march to your own drummer . . . "

It is this personal, individual pace which offers our lives stability. To exceed it, is to stir an inner frenzy. To fall behind this beat within you, is to cause the erosion of personal deterioration.

You can neither speed it up nor slow it down. It is your own muffled drum, your own inner rhythm, your own private pace.

Is conducting your life at your built-in pace a limitation?

Not unless stability is a limitation. Not unless poise and serenity and inner calm are limitations. And they are not.

In a world which buffets us about—sometimes gently, sometimes harshly—we would be at the mercy of relentless, unpredictable and disastrously varying forces, if we did not accept them calmly, knowing that we could proceed "in fortune and misfortune, at our own private pace, like the ticking of a clock in a thunderstorm."

Thus our lives maintain stability. It is this marching through life, unhurried and undisturbed, to the muffled beat of our inner drummer, in accord with our own rhythm, which enables us to keep on course, however the forces of chance may press against us.

To achieve this stability, to march through the vicissitudes of life with steady, even persistence requires, first, that we accept the existence of an inner rhythm which sets our inner pace. By living at the rate of our own inner pace, we find inner peace. It is a condition diligently to be sought.

But how to seek it? How to find it? That is much like asking how to find God. In fact, the two are interrelated—because rhythm is a part of the Universe.

Light is the result of rhythmic light waves. Sound is the result of rhythm sound waves. Electric power is the result of successive rhythmic impulses. The Universe consists of the vastness of planets rotating at a precise pace around their suns—huge demonstrations of their minimized reproductions in the infinite organization of all matter and energy. From the largest to the smallest components of Infinity there is repeated motion—a rhythm, a pace.

To recognize and accept this Universal truth, is to know that you—as a part of the Universe—have an inner pace, too. Awareness of its existence is prerequisite to finding it. It is not so obvious as the pace of your heartbeat or breathing, although these physical symptoms, together with your degree of tension, stress and strain, all are indicators of whether or not you are living in rhythm with your inner pace.

Just as a motor, the moving parts of which are not rhythmically synchronized, will destroy itself through the continuing shocks of excessive vibration—so you will destroy yourself if you do not live your life at the inner pace which produces inner calm.

And that is the test. If you do not normally maintain an inner calm, it is a warning that you are not—physically, mentally or spiritually—living in rhythm with your own inner pace.

Only you can make the necessary adjustments in your own life—but when you have made them, you will feel an inner calm . . . you will know the "peace that passeth understanding."

Chapter 52

The Ostrich Target

It has been said that an ostrich which sticks its head in the sand, makes an irresistible target for a paddle.

And so people who, ostrich-like, bend over to hide their heads in the sands of unreality, make irresistible targets for the paddle of Fate.

Which brings up the highly controversial subject of the positive affirmation which tries to hide like an ostrich from the reality of evil.

One cannot think of the generalized positive affirmation without thinking of the psychologist-psychiatrist Emile Coué and his famous affirmation, "Every day in every way I'm getting better and better." I can remember when a lot of people used to laugh at that. Well, they can stop laughing.

Emile Coué cured a lot of people by having them repeat that simple affirmation over and over again, in every spare minute, day after day. That was all—repeat it and believe it. That simple affirmation effected many remarkable cures and it will cure a lot of people today.

Since more than half of today's illnesses are psychosomatic (which, as you know, means bodily disorders induced by mental or emotional disturbances) it is clear that Emile Coué used one of various methods of treating the source of more than half of all illnesses and, in addition, provided a favorable mental and emotional attitude toward physically-caused diseases as well.

The use of the conscious mind to implant beneficial suggestions in the subconscious mind is an accepted form of therapy. It will be dealt with in other chapters of this book, but it is not the subject of this chapter.

Here we are to consider the insistence of Emile Coué on using the most general possible affirmation, "Every day in every way I'm getting better and better." Note how general and broad the terms of that affirmation are.

This wasn't because Coué was trying to reduce the therapy of affirmation to its simplest form. Nor was he seeking an all-purpose cure. He insisted on the use of broad, general, indefinite terms because he was afraid to be definite and name the specific ailments or diseases in the affirmations he had his patients implant in their subconscious minds.

For example, Coué would not permit his patients to use a specific affirmation such as, "Every day in every way my *sore back* is getting better and better." He was afraid that implanting an affirmation in the patient's subconscious mind specifying "*sore back*" would focus the subconscious on the ailment itself and thus aggravate it or, at least, perpetuate it. So his affirmation never referred to a specific condition.

Now, there is a lot of logic and sound psychology in Coué's reasoning. It generally is accepted that the subconscious mind is like an electronic computer. You feed information, visual images, emotional feelings, into it and consciously give it directions. Then, in cybernetic fashion, it steers the course of your life to bring into reality the mental images and directions of your conscious mind. It cannot judge whether they are good or bad, right or wrong. Its function is solely to materialize them as it interprets them.

Since the subconscious mind receives and "understands" only mental pictures, Coué reasoned that the inclusion of a specific ailment—such as "*sore back*"—in an affirmation which was impressed in the subconscious mind, would steer its course toward the physical realization, or, in this case the maintenance of, the ailment. Therefore in his affirmation, "Every day in every way I'm getting better and better," he avoided all mention of any specific ailments on the theory that if his patients got "better and better" their specific ailments also would get "better and better." He turned specifics into generalities and thereby avoided them. Ostrich-like.

Which brings us back to the ostrich with its head in the sand—and people who, ostrich-like, bend over to hide their heads in the sands of unreality, and thus make make irresistible targets to tempt a paddle-wielding Fate.

It seems to me unrealistic to deny the existence of evil. Or unhappiness. Or suffering. Or trouble. To do so is hiding our heads in the sand; we hide from no one and we escape from nothing.

This is no book on religion. I do not propose to have here a struggle between Good and Evil—nor a confrontation between God and the Devil.

I merely point out that evil and unhappiness and suffering and trouble DO exist; that there is evidence of them all around us, and that this evidence is undeniable. We cannot escape by hiding our heads in the sands of unreality nor can we make them less specific by generalizations in the manner of Emile Coue.

I, therefore, would like to suggest an alternate to the Coué approach of unspecific generalization. And not merely an alternate approach, but an opposite one:

(1) Clearly recognize and frankly ADMIT the existence of whatever trouble comes to you. Face up to it! Define it *specifically*. Confront it *precisely*.

(2) ACCEPT it! Not with defeatism and abject submission, but with the unflinching realism that it is so. There is no greater relief than the acceptance of reality. There is no greater torment than the futility of escapism.

(3) Having realistically accepted trouble—which you have defined *specifically*, so that you can attack it *precisely*—ACT! You have a *definite* trouble. You do not have to approach it in a *general* manner. You can strike at its *center*, where the *solution* is.

There you have the alternate to the ostrich escape from the reality of evil, unhappiness, suffering and the inevitable troubles that flesh is heir to.

You will not be immobilized, bent over, with your head, ostrich-like, stuck in the sand of escapism to present an irresistible target to the paddle of Fate. You will be on the move—and a moving target is harder to hit . . . even for Fate.

Therefore, this call for action!

The therapeutic and cybernetic values of *specific*, positive affirmation are multiplied many times when charged with the high voltage of *direct action*.

To consciously seek the attitudinal guidance of your subconscious, provides you with a rocket, fully-powered, and aimed directly at your goal.

But you must have *"lift-off"*!

You must *act*! Act with bold confidence in the goal-seeking guidance-system which is a part of your subconscious mind. Act in the knowledge that whatever man can *conceive* and *believe*—man can *achieve*.

So . . . seek no general "ostrich" cure; attack the *specific* cause, to surmount a *specific* difficulty.

Know that in the *doing*, you will be given the *power*!

Then *concentrate* that power!

And . . . let all ostriches beware!

Chapter 53

Include Yourself In

Having been president of a national advertising agency and a nationwide public relations firm before I retired, I'd like to pass along, for your consideration and possible use, a technique of "image building" not generally known by the public.

It is called: "Including yourself in."

It is applying the "we" attitude to yourself or your firm or group in association with "other leaders." Of course you must, in fact, be a leader of at least some consequence,or be worthy of consideration as a leader, to use the image-building technique of "including yourself in." Otherwise you will undermine your credibility, or even appear ridiculous.

But there are many people, firms and groups who would be included in and accepted by a group to which they deservedly could belong if they would always "include themselves in" and always say "we" in referring to such a group.

Let me give you a few examples of this very rewarding technique—starting with business firms. In our advertising and public relations work, we had various clients who were, at first, not considered to be among the leaders in their respective fields.

So in their advertising, publicity, and in their statements and actions, they "included themselves in" the next highest status bracket until they were accepted at the very top—if not for size, then for quality, or some other leadership "image".

Among the many techniques which can be used to "include yourself in" is the use of the word "we" to associate yourself in the public mind with well-known, fully-accepted leaders. Frequently assert: "As one of the leaders in this industry, we must share the responsibility for . . ." Or: "As a leader in this field, we are proud of the accomplishments which have been achieved in . . ." Or: "We know we cannot maintain our position of leadership in quality craftsmanship unless we continue to . . ."

In using this "include yourself in" technique, the meaning you give the word "we" is extremely important. For example, Negroes, in asserting racial equality, lose the opportunity to express integrated equality whenever they say: "we", meaning: "we, Negroes", when they should, in asserting racial equality, say: "we, citizens" . . . "we, parents" . . . "we, taxpayers" . . . "we, university graduates" . . . "we, Americans". By "including themselves in" integrated groups to which they certainly belong, they would stop emphasizing their differences and establish their similarity. Similarity is the road to acceptance. It "includes you in".

The technique, then, is to find similarities with the group with which you want to be identified, then use the inclusive word: "we" in describing yourself as a part of that group.

How others regard you—the "image" they have of you—is largely under your own control. "Image-building" is well worth the thought, planning and continuous effort it requires. Others will respect you and respond to you in direct accordance with the "image" you have built of yourself in their minds. Thus you, yourself, determine how others will treat you—for better or for worse.

Perhaps the most rewarding time you can spend is in deciding what you want to "be" in the judgment of others, giving full consideration to the consequences which will result. Then do whatever it takes to be indisputably *that,* being sure to "include yourself in" those groups, the accepted membership in which will establish your "image".

Do it conscientiously, do it honestly, do it well, and the "image" which you build will be real. It will be **YOU!**

Chapter 54

Smile . . . ANYHOW!!!

You probably have heard the story of the woman who was beset with annoyances, problems and troubles. So she lettered a sign reading: "Smile!" and fastened it to her bathroom mirror as a reminder. However, she still was beset with annoyances, problems and troubles, so she took down the sign reading: "Smile!"—and replaced it with a sign reading: "Smile . . . ANYHOW!!!"

No one is immune to annoyances, problems and troubles. They are a part of life and, while we may not enjoy them, they do keep life from being a dull routine. Just think how boring it would be to sit in a rocking chair and eat chocolate ice cream all day!

Fortunately for each of us, there is more to life than a rocking chair and ice cream existence. Irritations with which to cope, problems to be solved, obstacles to be overcome, challenges to be met—all act as stimulants, and if we don't find life stimulating, we shall not find it interesting.

Psychologists have offered various suggestions to get us "part of the action", as the current expression goes.

One psychologist prescribes: "Always have a fight on!" He emphasizes that the fight should be for a worthy cause, or against injustice, poverty, disease. I have a friend who is a retired sales manager. His fight is for the conservation of this nation's natural resources and wildlife. He is devoting his retirement and his considerable talent to fighting for a worthy cause. He eagerly takes on all comers—including me! While I agree with and encourage almost all of his conservation activities, I once wrote him, disagreeing with a statement he had made in one of his national newsletters, which he finances privately. He promptly published, with my permission, my two-page, fully-documented letter of criticism! Think he finds life dull? He always has a fight on! He *likes* problems! He can "Smile . . . ANYHOW!!!"

To meet the annoyances and problems of life and "Smile . . . ANYHOW!!!", psychologists prescribe: "Grapple!" There is a chapter on "Grapple" in this book (Chapter 40) which I suggest you re-read in full, so I shall only briefly review it here. Mental and emotional illness is caused by the overwhelming accumulation of unsolved problems. To prevent excess anxiety, avoid this accumulation of problems by meeting each problem as it arises and enthusiastically grappling with it until you reach a satisfactory solution. (Note: I said: "satisfactory solution", not "the one, best, perfect solution".) It requires as much energy to try to escape from a problem as it does to grapple with it and solve it. So take the psychologists' advice and solve your problems by enthusiastically grappling with them.

Then, when you have a problem, you can "Smile . . . ANYHOW!!!"

That is the key to enjoying life, even with its daily quota of irritations and problems. Smile . . . ANY-HOW!!! Anybody can smile when everything goes right —the secret is to be able to smile when everything goes wrong. You, like all the rest of us, are going to have your share of annoyances, problems and troubles—so you might just as well decide to take them in your stride and smile at them as unwelcome, but inevitable, visitors. It isn't what happens, but how you feel about what happens, that really counts. And you *can* control your feeling.

According to the eminent authority, William James, you can control your feeling by acting the way you want to feel. So if you want to feel happier—smile! Even if you don't have a reason to smile—"Smile . . . ANY-HOW!!!"

And since a fair share of your life, like all lives, will be made up of annoyances, problems and troubles, do what the wise woman at the beginning of this chapter did. Take down your reminder sign which reads: "Smile!"—and realistically replace it with a sign which reminds you to: "Smile . . . ANYHOW!!!"

Chapter 55

How To Be A Billionaire

It is the serious purpose of this chapter to tell you how to make a BILLION dollars. Now that sounds like a lot of money. And it is. Specifically it is 1,000 million dollars.

The only sure way to learn how to make a billion dollars is to learn from a billionaire. There is no point in taking advice from someone who hasn't done it.

The following instructions on how to make a billion dollars come from J. Paul Getty whose assets exceed one and one-half billion dollars (more than 1,500 millionaires).

I witnessed an interview with billionaire J. Paul Getty during which he was asked the secret of his success. Here is his billion-dollar secret in two words:

"TRY HARDER!"

That's it. Just TRY HARDER. If that seems too simple, think it through to its ultimate conclusion.

First you try harder . . . and then you try harder than that . . . and you try harder than that . . . then try harder than that . . . and so you pyramid your efforts and you pyramid your gains.

Compounded effort is like compound interest—it expands at a terrific rate. Pyramiding your efforts is like pyramiding your profits—the acceleration in your gains is enormous and the total result . . . well, Paul Getty made one and one-half billion dollars!

His method: TRY HARDER!

I happen to have devoted my life to studying success techniques. I have three personal libraries of books explaining how to be successful. I have documented the success methods of all the most successful men and women in the world. I have fifteen private files of more than 1,000 proven success methods. I have recorded these success methods in a series of books which are sold separately but which, together, comprise the complete *Proven Success Methods Library* described on the back of this book's jacket. My purpose has been to enable everyone to achieve success whatever his or her present situation.

Now along comes a billionaire who tells how to succeed, in just two words: "TRY HARDER".

The more I think about Paul Getty's advice, the more I like it as a life slogan . . . TRY HARDER.

Chapter 56

GOODWILL Is Your SUCCESS INSURANCE

You insure your life, health, income, property and just about everything valuable, the loss of which would be a disaster to you and your family. You wisely add insurance as necessary.

But do you, just as prudently, acquire SUCCESS INSURANCE? And do you constantly add to your SUCCESS INSURANCE?

Success Insurance is usually called by a more familiar name . . . GOODWILL.

Just because the concept of goodwill is familiar, do not pass it by lightly. Goodwill may be or may become one of your most valuable assets. In addition to its many other satisfactions, goodwill has a very high monetary value. In the sale or merger of businesses, their goodwill has a definite dollars-and-cents value which, in many transactions, amounts to millions of dollars.

In some businesses, goodwill is their greatest single asset. Many companies have been purchased for huge sums primarily to acquire the goodwill associated with their famous names or the popular brand names of their products.

Individuals, of course, acquire goodwill, too, and it can have great monetary value. But the purpose of this chapter is to consider goodwill as your personal SUCCESS INSURANCE and, in this context, goodwill is not purchased but must be created by what you say, write or do.

Remember those three words: "say, write or do" because they will be the basis of a simple test which will guide you in creating the personal SUCCESS INSURANCE of goodwill.

First, to assure you of the importance and value of this test, I want to relate my own experience with it. Having retired at fifty, after a business career which included being president of eight corporations, I have devoted some of my retirement to analyzing the causes of my successes and failures, to provide some first-hand material to be included in a compact library of Success Books which I am writing.

My post-analysis revealed that what I did right and what I did wrong, in almost *every* instance, was substantially determined by whether I succeeded or failed to meet the requirements of this simple test; although, unfortunately, I did not know about this test, as such, at the time. I wish I had.

Any test which has so much to do with success or failure—and which, if used, will *insure* your success—should have your most careful consideration. I am emphasizing the word "*insure*" because insurance presupposes the existence of other elements and factors; therefore, other ingredients of success must also be present—but, if they are, this test will provide the *insurance* factor.

Here is your SUCCESS INSURANCE test:

(1) In dealing with others, do not say, write or do *anything* until you have asked yourself this simple question: "Will what I am about to say, write or do—create *goodwill* or incur *ill will*?"

(2) If you can answer with asssurance that what you are about to say, write or do, will create *goodwill* (and the other necessary success factors also are present), *do it.*

(3) But if you thoughtfully conclude that what you are about to say, write or do, will incur *ill will* (no matter how clever, expedient or even "justified" it may be) . . . *do not do it.*

It is difficult to resist being clever, or doing what is expedient, or responding in kind to an insult, or unnecessarily proving that you are right or are smarter than some other person, or doing so many of the self-satisfying things which injure the precious ego of another to please or even placate your own ego. But it is much more difficult for you to overcome the immediate or future damage of the *ill will* which you thus incur.

It is a sinister characteristic of ill will to seem innocuous at its inception only to escalate to major proportions as it becomes emotionalized by repeated reviewing. Make it a rule: *never incur ill will.* Your own ego satisfaction just isn't worth it.

Now let's consider the SUCCESS INSURANCE of GOODWILL. This is goodwill which you, yourself, must create in your relations with others. It requires thought, effort and often the expenditure of some of your money. Obtaining the goodwill of others does not just happen. It is the direct result of something you say, write or do deliberately to create their goodwill toward you. It seldom is spontaneous. Your SUCCESS INSURANCE must be planned as carefully as you plan your other insurance.

That is because drawing the goodwill of others toward you is the result of your giving others a *bonus*, of your giving them something *extra—something which they want*—which is neither required nor expected, but which you give freely, willingly, graciously. And it must be clear that you expect nothing in return but their *goodwill.*

That is the key! Give something *extra—a bonus* —to others, which they have no right to require or even to expect, and for which it is clear you want nothing in return except *goodwill.*

Naturally, the something extra—the bonus—you give others must be *something they want* or it will be worse than valueless in terms of building goodwill.

So, how can you be sure that you are giving others a bonus of what they want? Well, we return again to those three invisible signs everybody wears across his or her chest:

(1) I want to be IMPORTANT.

(2) I want to be ADMIRED.

(3) I want to be APPRECIATED.

If in dealing with others, whatever you say, write or do, gives others an *extra* feeling of deserved importance, an *extra* satisfaction of being genuinely admired, a *bonus* of sincere appreciation, substantially exceeding that which could be required or even expected—then you can be sure that you have added to their goodwill toward you and thus have added to your SUCCESS INSURANCE.

How, specifically, can you do this? What other ways are there to create goodwill? How much thought, time, effort and money should you devote to creating goodwill, acquiring SUCCESS INSURANCE?

Each person's situation is different. You are in a better position to answer these questions for yourself than I am. And, anyway, the purpose of this book is to start you into channels of rewarding thoughts—not to do your thinking for you, even if I could, and I cannot.

But I can conceive of no more rewarding "THOUGHTS TO BUILD ON" than for you to plan exactly how you will create more *goodwill* in each and every present and future personal relationship . . . and thereby *insure your success* in life.

Chapter 57

Use Your NOTHING COMPUTER

A very valuable computer has just been discovered!

This valuable computer has been discovered *inside* YOU!

It is called the NOTHING COMPUTER.

It is called the NOTHING COMPUTER because it does absolutely *nothing* about whatever problems are fed into it. You just feed into your NOTHING COMPUTER all of your problems, anxieties, fears, resentments, and all the other unpleasantness about which you cannot do anything constructive—you assign them to your NOTHING COMPUTER and let it do the unnecessary worrying for you—while you devote your constructive thought and effort to worthwhile accomplishments.

Most of us are partially immobilized by the memories of our mistakes in countless yesterdays. Yet we cannot re-live the past. So why bear these additional burdens? Put them into your NOTHING COMPUTER.

Let go of them. Let your NOTHING COMPUTER handle your remorse and regrets.

Many of us live in anxiety and sometimes panic concerning the future. Yet we cannot see beyond the hands of today's clock. So why burden yourself with imagined events which have not even occurred, may never happen, and cannot be dealt with before their time? Put them into your NOTHING COMPUTER. And leave them there.

Sufficient unto each day are the tasks thereof. We have enough difficulty with today's tasks, without adding the remorse of the past and the anxiety of the future. So irrevocably put your past regrets and future worries into your NOTHING COMPUTER—and they will not return to disturb you, because your NOTHING COMPUTER will keep them locked inside, while diligently working on them by doing . . . *nothing!*

Anything which would disturb, annoy, worry or burden you—and which you cannot, should not, or do not choose to do anything about, should be turned over to your NOTHING COMPUTER with the feeling of relief that you have entirely disposed of that annoyance.

Remember, annoyances will not go away of their own accord. You have to *do* something to dispose of them. The conclusive way to dispose of them is to assign them to your NOTHING COMPUTER.

A few examples:

Unlike Will Rogers, who claimed he never met a man he did not like, I have met people whom, for valid reasons, I did not like. But their continued existence on this same planet does not disturb me in the least. You see,

I have assigned them to my NOTHING COMPUTER. And . . . good riddance!

There was a man who had a constantly complaining wife. Yet he was serenely undisturbed by her petty complaints; they never reached his consciousness because he sent them directly to his NOTHING COMPUTER.

There was a wife whose husband had a quick temper. She did not over-react to his brief anger and thus precipitate a shouting match resulting in mutually hurt feelings. She simply assigned his temper tantrums to her NOTHING COMPUTER. Since he could not argue with nothing and found himself threshing around in an emotional vacuum, he learned to feed the various causes of his irritability into his own NOTHING COMPUTER and thus had nothing to be angry about.

A NOTHING COMPUTER is simply an amusing, imaginary device for accomplishing what psychiatrists call "catharsis" (which, in common parlance, means "getting rid of undesirable thoughts and feelings"), and a NOTHING COMPUTER also provides the means of mentally and emotionally "blanking out" undesirable thoughts and feelings so that they do not make a conscious, much less a subconscious, impression on you.

To be able to eliminate all mental-emotional reactions to undesirable thoughts and feelings is a state of perfection constantly to be sought. In the meantime, at least discipline yourself not to *over-react* in any situation.

OVER-REACTING will get you into serious trouble—*fast!* Serious trouble cannot be handled by your useful, amusing, imaginary NOTHING COMPUTER. But serious trouble can be handled calmly, intelligently by RESTRAINING OVER-REACTION.

In addition to the professional warnings of psychiatrists, psychologists, personality counselors and many others concerned with personal problems, there are numerous homespun admonitions against *over-reacting* which have come down through the years, such as:

"Don't burn down the barn to kill the rats."

"Don't put out a small fire with a big bucket of water."

And, we might include a more modern one for college rioters, "Don't close the college to spite the School Board."

OVER-REACTION in ANGER probably will hurt you emotionally more than the enemy you surely will make. By pouring the gasoline of over-reaction in anger on the temporary flickering flames of displeasure, you start an inferno of hate which escalates with each additional bucket of gasoline. And, you make conciliation more difficult, if not impossible. Your anger will continue to burn long after your target has shrugged you off as an undisciplined, uncontrolled hot-head.

OVER-REACTION in GRIEF cuts even deeper into the emotional wound and sets up a complex network of deep memory patterns which are so sensitive that even unrelated future events trigger renewed sorrow. Since grief is the reaction to an irreplaceable loss, OVER-REACTION in GRIEF cannot replace the loss, but serves only to escalate the pain of sorrow, providing neither comfort nor consolation.

OVER-REACTION in JOY seems to be a sort of super-happy experience which constructively accents the positive in contrast to the negative impact and damaging results of over-reacting in anger and grief. It has been recommended by such philosophical statements as, "When once the cup of pleasure is to your lips, drink it to the dregs; it may not come again." Yet it is wise not to over-react even to joy because as Longfellow said, "Not enjoyment and not sorrow is our destined end or way." So do as Kipling advised: "Meet with triumph and disaster and treat those two imposters just the same." Only by such even-handedness can you maintain psychiatrist Dr. Karl Menninger's requirement of "Vital Balance."

The wise men insistently are telling us that the pendulum of Life swings back and forth. And, the psychiatrists say that our reactions determine both extremes of its arc. The pleasure-pain graph-line of Life goes up and down, but we may control its peaks and valleys by the extent of our reaction or over-reaction to the direction of its movement.

We should curb OVER-REACTION and extremism in *any* direction—and seek, instead, psychiatrist Dr. Karl Menninger's "Vital Balance" as a way to equanimity—for only in calmness and serenity will we find peace of mind.

Chapter 58

Permissiveness Makes Slobs

The permissive persuaders have had their say.

Now it's time someone spoke up for discipline. Physical discipline. Mental discipline. Moral discipline.

Start with physical discipline. I cannot think of any noteworthy physical accomplishment which has been achieved without physical discipline. Ask any athlete. Better still, ask any champion. Only the most constant discipline can produce the physique, the stamina, the co-ordination—the complete physical ability—to be a champion.

But you don't aspire to be a champion? Then choose your niche. The choice is up to you. Depending on how soon in life you start, you can attain whatever physical perfection your remaining years allow—or through physical permissiveness, hit skid row. Or, choose any degree of physical fitness in between.

It's simply a matter of physical discipline—based on information. The facts of physical fitness are simple and easy to learn. So it is really a matter of doing what you *must* do and not doing what you *must not* do. That's discipline. It's not always fun. Sometimes it's disagreeable. Sometimes it's just plain rough. But it pays off big in results. Much better than physical permissiveness. Because physical permissiveness will make you a slob.

Even so, physical discipline is easier than mental discipline. Somehow it's harder to keep your mind under control than your body. That's because, in evolution, man's body developed before his mind. In fact, man's mind hasn't developed very much yet. The day's news is ample evidence of that.

There is a great excess of mental permissiveness: mental wandering, aimless, uncontrolled, undisciplined.

Of course, there is a great deal of subconscious mental wandering during sleep. It is a phenomenon which should not be left to Freud. The opportunities for constructive use of the time thus spent every night are too great. Research, to date, has accomplished too little. Yet the problem is so complex, we must leave it to the specialists.

However, there is much we can do about mental discipline during our waking hours. And there is much we need to do. For example, take concentration. Can you concentrate on just one simple, single thought without another thought interrupting for fifteen seconds? For thirty seconds? For a minute? Try it.

Without the mental discipline of controlled concentration, we accomplish only a slight fraction of what we could. Controlled concentration can be attained by anybody. It is a matter of mental discipline. Practice. Training.

Even more important is our disciplined control of *what* we think. Because *what* we think determines substantially what we *are* and specifically what we shall *become.*

"As a man *thinketh* . . . so *is* he", says the Bible.

Buddha taught, "All that we *are* is the result of what we have *thought.*"

Throughout all great religions, throughout all significant philosophies, throughout the personal disciplines of all great individuals, is the dominant assertion that each of us *is* or *becomes* the materialization of what he *thinks.*

This process of being or becoming what we think, is accelerated by the intensity of our deeply believing what we think.

The Bible says, "ALL things are possible to him that *believeth.*" That's a strong statement, but it comes from the Source of the possible—God.

Study the miracle cures and you will find *one* cause—deep belief. Some day we shall discover that miracles are not miraculous at all—just happenings which we do not, at the time, understand. Miracles are *caused,* and the cause is deep belief.

Study the lives of great men and women, and you will discover that underlying each great achievement was the immovable foundation of deep belief in their personal abilities, in their ultimate success. *Psychologists have proven that whatever the mind can conceive and believe—man can achieve.*

William James taught that: "BELIEF CREATES THE ACTUAL FACT." He said, "In any project, the important factor is your *belief*. Without *belief* there can be no successful outcome. That is fundamental."

Belief is the result of a *disciplined* mind. Only a disciplined mind can concentrate the intensity of belief into the white heat of a desire powerful enough to achieve its goal. So William James further taught: "If you only *care enough* for a result, you will almost certainly attain it. If you wish to be rich, you will be rich; if you wish to be learned, you will be learned; if you wish to be good, you will be good. Only you must, then, *really* wish these things, and wish them exclusively, and not wish at the same time a hundred other incompatible things just as strongly." Mental focus through *mental discipline.*

Dr. Walter Scott, famous psychologist and President of Northwestern University, taught: "Success or failure in business is caused more by *mental attitudes* than by mental capacities." Mental attitudes are the result of *mental discipline.*

The famous preacher-psychologist-writer, Dr. Norman Vincent Peale, says: "Think success, visualize success, and you will set in motion the power-force of the realizable wish. When the mental picture or attitude is *strongly enough held,* it actually seems to control conditions and circumstances." To hold a mental picture or attitude *strongly enough* requires *mental discipline.*

Finally, let's take our case for *mental discipline* all the way to the U.S. Supreme Court. The decision . . . by the late Justice Cardozo: "We *are* what we *believe* we are." To believe deeply and constantly requires *mental discipline.* Case closed.

Probably it is in the field of morals that the persuaders of permissiveness have most deeply damaged humanity. Their reasoning is so subtle and their teaching so appealing: "Be free! Turn on and do whatever you want to do! Tune out and ignore whatever you do not want to do! Disregard any moral discipline which limits your lust. Disobey any law with which you do not agree. Moral permissiveness will set you free!"

Yes, permissiveness will make you free—as free as a truck loaded with explosives free-wheeling down a steep, winding mountain road . . . *without brakes!*

And permissiveness will do something else for you. *Permissiveness—physical, mental and moral permissiveness—will make you a* SLOB!

Chapter 59

The Crystal Globe

I would like to send a globe to each Great Man of each Great Nation.

It would be a globe of the Earth. Except it would show no nations and no continents. Neither land nor sea. Only a clear, crystal globe—like a crystal ball—to place on his desk near the red push-button.

Just something to look at . . . as his finger toys with the little red push-button near by. Perhaps he will see in his crystal ball . . .

Blossoms of babies, soft in their cribs. A tiny boy gaily pulling an even more tiny girl in a little red wagon. A group of youngsters giggling. And older teen-agers who have stopped giggling because of the seriousness of it all. A bride and groom in their great moment at the altar. Men at work, building, building—for what? Women, when their own day's work is done, waiting for their men to come home and take them in their arms. An old couple sitting side by side, holding hands as they did in their yesterdays and silently praying that there will be more tomorrows.

Perhaps each Great Man of each Great Nation will see these in his crystal ball, and then it will be clear crystal again. Merely a blank globe of the Earth . . . no nations and no continents . . . neither land nor sea . . . as his finger toys with the red push-button.

Chapter 60

The Lesson Of The Butterfly

I stood quietly in the field of new-mown hay and watched a beautiful butterfly as it fluttered frantically about . . . searching . . . seeking . . . wanting.

Only yesterday the butterfly had found the flower. And it had become a very special flower to the butterfly. To be sought. To be near. To be gently caressed as only a beautiful butterfly can caress a lovely flower.

But the flower had not been special to the mower. And it lay cut and wilting in the noonday sun, half-hidden in the cut grass. No longer lovely.

Poor butterfly! Fluttering frantically about . . . searching . . . seeking . . . wanting.

So we learn in life's hard school that the goals which we cherished yesterday meant nothing to life's mower today and we find them cut down and wilting among the cut grasses at our feet.

But as the butterfly keeps searching . . . seeking . . . wanting . . . it will find other lovelier flowers.

And so must we seek new and greater goals. For we shall find them if we seek, just as the butterfly will find more and lovelier flowers.

As in the world of butterflies, there is an abundance of flowers—so in our own lives there is an abundance of goals, each with a greater reward than that which seemed so essential before life, with a wisdom we are not meant to understand, cut it down.

It's life's way of keeping us ever searching . . . and seeking . . . and wanting. In so doing, we learn the purpose of the mower . . . which cuts down our yesterdays so that we may seek and find an even brighter tomorrow.

Chapter 61

Which Way Do You Lean?

In a vocabulary of larger words, I would have to say this is a chapter about predisposition. But by preference, I'd like to write a bit about *leaning*, which is a simpler way of saying it.

You see, leaning is important—the direction in which you lean, that is. Not north nor south nor east nor west, but depending upon the direction from which comes each storm of life.

Always lean *into* the storms of life. Lean *toward* danger—never away from it.

There are those who will tell you to lean *with* life's winds so their forces will not break you. Give way, they say. Bend with the forces, even to lying prone, and let the storms of life pass over you to seek more hardy victims. Then, when all is calm again, you can struggle to your feet and brush your clothes—and smile smugly to yourself, reassured that you haven't been hurt.

You haven't been hurt? Well, for one thing, your character has been hurt! And that mysterious thing inside you, known as your subconscious, has been predisposed to bending with each blow, to giving way to each force, even to lying down in the hope that danger will pass over you to seek out someone else.

And that first time you gave way in the face of life's storm, you judged yourself, and sealed the verdict deep inside you—that you were a coward. Then the next time and the next, you knew which way you would lean. The same way always: *away* from danger.

This leaning away, this allowing yourself to bend with each passing storm of life—what does it matter? Can you not stand straight again when the danger is past? Well, not exactly straight, because, you see, your character will be bent.

This results in more than just a sense of inner insecurity, of anxious anticipation of the next storm to lean away from. It brands you. Then everyone will know which way you will lean in danger. It will show in your eyes—and in your attitudes. Yes, people will know and judge and respond to how you will lean.

A Chinese sage of long ago said wisely, "Everybody pushes a falling fence".

And so they do. In derision, I suppose, because the falling fence leans away from whatever pushed it. Ready to lean some more whenever it is pushed again. Like some people!

Those who have watched a herd of animals can easily tell the leader. Animals can sense impending danger and *always,* without the slightest hesitation, the *leader* of the herd moves *toward* the *danger.* Or he would no longer be accepted as leader. He is instinctively predisposed to place himself between the herd and danger. He leans *toward* danger. Therefore, he is the unquestioned *leader.*

That is the mark of a leader of people. When all the debate is finished, when all the other tests have been given, there is just one final test which, in the end, determines the ultimate decision: Are you, by instinct—or even better, by training—predisposed to *always,* without the slightest hestitation, place yourself between your people and danger? When the storms of life reach the force to push you around, do you resolutely lean *into* every storm—and stand firm?

That is the ultimate mark of leadership.

That is the ultimate test of your quality as a person.

Chapter 62

You Can Live Twice

Sir Christopher Wren lived in the seventeenth century.

In fact, he lived TWICE in the seventeenth century!

His first life consisted of growing up, getting a good education and being a professor of astronomy at Gresham College and Oxford. That first life lasted forty-eight years. Then he decided "he had done that" and there wasn't any particular point in continued repetition.

So he decided he would live a new and entirely different life. He decided that instead of being an astronomer and just looking at a distant heaven, he would bring Heaven down to earth by building beautiful churches and majestic cathedrals.

After his first life of forty-eight years as a scholar and teacher, Sir Christopher Wren devoted a second life of forty-one years to building fifty-three churches and cathedrals of such beauty and grandeur that they stand as monuments to his greatness. He designed and supervised the building of the magnificent St. Paul's Cathedral in London for which he will be forever famous.

Of course, you can be prosaic about it and say Sir Christopher merely changed professions. But I like to think of him as living a different and second life. Like the man James Whitcomb Riley wrote about, who said that now that he had lived his full three score and ten, he had finally got the hang of living and therefore proposed to do it over again—only do it better.

So, Sir Christopher Wren really lived a second and different life—and lived it better.

This is not unusual. Lots of people have done it. I mention it only to point up the wisdom in the advice one hears more and more these days: "DON'T GET STUCK WITH THE PRESENT!"

There was a man who lived four different lives! His name was Dr. Albert Schweitzer. As a Doctor of Philosophy he was the author of many learned books. A fulfilling life in itself!

Then he sought a new life in religion. He studied theology and earned a Doctor's degree in that subject. He became Curate of St. Nicholas Church in Strasbourg and there began a different and second life.

But even two rewarding lives were not enough for Dr. Schweitzer. He loved beautiful music, so he studied it, mastered it, and earned a Doctor's degree in music. He went on to become one of the greatest concert organists of all time!

Having achieved fame and acclaim in his life of music, Dr. Schweitzer felt a compelling desire to minister to the poor and the sick savages of the jungles of Africa. So he began to study to be a physician and surgeon. Finally he earned his fourth Doctor's degree, this time in medicine. He gave up his life of fame and acclaim as a great concert organist to begin a fourth and totally different life in Lamborene, in steaming, tropical Africa, where his small group made a clearing in a giant forest infested with danger: pythons, gorillas, crocodiles, wild savages. There he built his "hospital" and lived the life he most wanted to live. There he found the divine greatness of a life based on the eternal lesson: "It is more blessed to give than to receive."

Most people live only one life and many have a difficult time making a success of that. Certainly it is better to continue doing what you do best and what brings the greatest good to others as well as to yourself. Change for the sake of change brings more frustration than happiness.

But neither do you have to give your allotted years to a life of dullness and mediocrity. In that case, you will do better to start all over again and live another and different life.

Just remember, you don't have to be "STUCK WITH THE PRESENT".

Chapter 63

Bad Temper Is Worse Than Bad Fortune

With good humor and a pleasant disposition you can conquer misfortune. But a bad temper and a nasty disposition will conquer you. A bad temper will make life a hell for you and all those around you.

There must be something very damaging about a bad temper because so many famous thinkers have made a special point of warning about it.

A bad temper will hurt you far more than it will hurt those at whom it is directed, as the English author, Charles Buxton warns, "Bad temper is its own scourge. Few things are more bitter than to feel bitter. A man's venom poisons himself more than his victim."

Or, as Bishop Richard Cumberland said, "Of all bad things by which mankind are cursed, their own bad tempers surely are the worst." Now, a Bishop has made ample study of "all bad things by which mankind are cursed." It is in the nature of the clergy's service to mankind, to consider the many ills that flesh is heir to, and to provide such alleviation or solace as is within the province of religion. Having thoughtfully considered the curses of mankind, Bishop Cumberland concluded that "their own bad tempers surely are the worst."

He is joined by other great thinkers of the Faith. The forthright Irish clergyman, Robert Clayton, stated bluntly, "If religion does nothing for your temper, it has done nothing for your soul."

And the English clergyman, Richard Cecil, added this advice, "If a man has a quarrelsome temper, let him alone." Which Dale Carnegie said another way when he wrote, "Never get into a squirting match with a skunk."

So if you want to feel lonely, if you want to be avoided and shunned, just develop and display a bad temper. Your instant success in the field of loneliness will be assured.

But your success will be limited to achieving loneliness; your bad temper will not make you welcome in the business world, for as the Earl of Chesterfield said, "A man who cannot command his temper should not think of being a man of business." To which we can add the advice of author Charles Cherbuliez, "Men who have had a great deal of experience learn not to lose their tempers."

What would you pay to learn the secret of finding happiness and avoiding misery? Well, you don't have to pay anything, and it isn't a secret, either. It was clearly stated way back in the seventeenth century by

Francois Rochefoucauld, "The happiness and misery of people depend on their tempers." And re-stated by the English philosopher, Earl of Shaftebury, "From temper only, a man may be completely miserable, let his outward circumstances be ever so fortunate."

Having quoted an English philosopher on the subject of temper, let's see what a German philosopher had to say. The famed Friedrich Nietzsche wrote, "The growth of wisdom may be gauged accurately by the decline of ill temper." And the wise Chinese philosopher, Lao-tse, listed gentleness as the first quality of greatness.

If we haven't the wisdom and the will power to get rid of our bad tempers and all the woes which accompany them, perhaps we will grow more agreeable as we grow older. "Not so!," says the American author, Washington Irving, "A tart temper never mellows with age; and a sharp tongue is the only edged tool that grows keener with constant use."

Mellowing with age may apply to wine, but if we expect it to apply to people—especially people who persist in indulging their bad tempers—we are in for a rude awakening. Aging does not reverse our personality characteristics—it intensifies and hardens them. This is especially true of bad tempers and irritable dispositions.

This is due to the psychological fact that the display of bad temper is an emotional habit and must be treated and cured as a habit. As Dr. Karl A. Menninger, one of America's foremost psychiatrists, points out in his excellent book, "The Human Mind", the display of bad temper is an infantile reaction carried over into adolescence and adult life. Originally venting temper was used as a means of obtaining an objective; later the bad temper was retained, not so much to attain minor objectives, which could not likely be obtained by this method, but because bad temper had become an emotional habit or pattern.

Dr. Menninger adds that the bad temper habit, with increased irascibility and irritability, may be activated by the drinkng of alcoholic beverages. So if you have a bad temper and a tendency to become irascible and irritable, don't think that a few drinks will make you a genial companion.

But bad temper is just one side of the coin. The other side is good temper—and there is just as much good in good temper as there is bad in bad temper. So let us go to the wise men and again ponder their thoughts.

We'll find a lot of encouragement in the words of the distinguished English author, Sir Arthur Helps, "More than half the difficulties of the world would be allayed or removed by the exhibition of good temper." If Sir Arthur had lived a century later and had witnessed the virulent, ill tempered denunciations which are routine at the United Nations, he would have insisted that his words be emblazoned in the assembly room.

Are you sick? Afflicted? Deformed? Or do you know anyone who is? Then listen to Joseph Addison, the English essayist, "A cheerful temper will lighten sickness and affliction, and render deformity itself agreeable."

Ladies, as you grow older, how much face cream do you use? Frankly, I think wrinkles are greatly to be admired—especially if they are the lines of fine character and personality. But, having been unble to convince any woman or any cosmetic manufacturer, I shall offer an alternate solution. It comes from Tatler and says, "Good humor and complacency of temper outlive all charms of a fine face and make the decays of it invisible." So there you have the ultimate in wrinkle-vanishing-creme!

And now . . . one final and happy thought . . . from author Washington Irving, "Good temper, like a sunny day, sheds brightness over everything!"

Let there be bright!

Chapter 64

When Everything Else Fails...

Here is a sure-cure for just about everything that ails you: failure, worry, discouragement, all psychosomatic illnesses, poverty—you name it—and this remedy will cure it!

What's more, it will cure your troubles even when everything else fails—*especially* when everything else fails! And this sure-cure always is ready for your instant use. It has helped so many millions of users, you at least ought to try it yourself . . .

When everything else fails . . . TRY HARD WORK!

Let's look at some examples. Let's start with failure. Not just any failure, but the man who failed more than anyone else in the world.

His name was Thomas Edison. He failed more than anyone else, because he tried more than anyone else, so naturally, he knew more things that wouldn't work. With that kind of information, he could (by working 18 hours a day) eventually find what would work, so he succeeded more than anyone else. In fact, he succeeded so well that he patented 1,093 inventions.

He said that genius is 1% inspiration and 99% perspiration—and he provided the perspiration by working 18 hours a day. He worked ten years to invent the nickel-iron-alkaline storage battery. He and his staff tested and classified 17,000 varieties of plants before they succeeded in extracting latex in substantial quantities from just one of them.

Would *you* be willing to work 18 hours a day and fail 17,000 times before you succeeded once? Maybe you aren't failing often enough—or working hard enough!

Are you providing the necessary 99% perspiration? There is no record of anyone being drowned in sweat.

But you can drown your *worries* in sweat! As a matter of fact, hard work is a sure cure for worry. It cures worry in three ways:

(1) If you work hard enough and concentrate exclusively on the job at hand, you will have neither time nor thought for worry.

(2) If you work hard enough, you'll go to bed and go to sleep, too tired to stay awake and worry.

(3) If you work hard enough and intelligently enough, you'll solve your problems so you won't have anything to worry about.

Are you discouraged? When everything else fails . . . TRY HARD WORK! Idle bodies and idle minds create a vacuum which discouragement is all too ready to fill.

There was a man who sat around doing nothing except worrying about his problems. The more he worried about them, the more discouraged he became, until finally he decided to commit suicide.

He didn't want his family and friends to know that he was a quitter and had "chickened out" on the problems of life, so he decided he would cause a natural heart attack by running around the block until he dropped dead.

So he started running . . . and he ran . . . and ran. The longer he ran, the more tired he got. In fact, he became so completely exhausted that he couldn't feel anything but sheer exhaustion. All he could think about was going to bed—which he did. He spent twelve hours in dreamless, perfectly relaxed sleep. And he awoke refreshed, feeling great, rarin' to take on any problem which dared challenge him!

But suppose you're ill. You hurt here and you hurt there, or you have this symptom or that. You really do. There's nothing imaginary about it. Even if your doctor can't find any physical cause. That simply means your illness is psychosomatic (mentally-emotionally caused, instead of physical). More than 50% of all ailments are. Some doctors say 90%. Anyway, you are just as ill from psychosomatic causes—only the treatment is different. Your doctor can cure you, except in the few cases which need a specialist. Usually you can cure yourself. With your doctor's permission, of course, TRY HARD WORK!

This cure-all for just about whatever ails you, also is highly effective in curing poverty. Its curative powers are recorded in many impressive testimonials. Let's consider a few cases of poor people:

For example, poor Andrew Carnegie. What? Andrew Carnegie, poor? Why he was the greatest steel tycoon! He made so many millions he couldn't give his money away fast enough, even though he endowed free public libraries in cities all over this nation. Well, Andrew Carnegie was so poor he had to start work at $4.00 a month!

Note the preceding words: "start *work*", for *hard work* was Carnegie's cure for his poverty—honest, concentrated, *hard work*. He said so himself: "Concentration is my motto—first honesty, then industry (*hard work*), then concentration". So as we seek to eliminate poverty, let us not overlook the advice of the man who started *work* at $4.00 a month and by honest, concentrated *hard work* became one of the richest of all.

John D. Rockefeller, who later became one of the richest men in the world, started *working* for $6.00 a week. And Henry Ford started *working* for $2.50 a week. Their fortunes were the result of *hard work*—as almost all great fortunes are.

I have devoted a lifetime to the study of success; not just financial success, but how people, under all sorts of conditions, were able to attain their goals in life. I have three personal libraries of books on the subject. So I can save your having to do a lot of research on success by assuring you that the only *sure* way to succeed is by *hard work*.

I write this with the full knowledge that the trend today is to try to get more and more money for less and less work. Certainly, I am for modernization, mechanization, automation and computerization. But these should *produce more* and *better* products and services at *lower prices* so that they may benefit *more,* and eventually *all,* people. To do this will require more work—not less work—by this generation and many generations to come.

When more than half of the people in the world do not have even enough to eat, when most of the people of the world do not have *any* of the conveniences which a small percentage of us in the "affluent society" take for granted—we have a big job to do, and it is going to take *hard work* to do it, even with the use of our computerized automation.

And we had better start now, not just for the good of humanity, but for our *own* good! Some day—*soon*—this drive to be paid more and more for working less and less is going to run head on into the Law of Diminishing Returns. When we price ourselves out of the world market, we will have priced our labor out of jobs and our industry out of business. Already foreign industry is producing many better products at much lower prices. Already our larger industries are building many more plants in foreign countries to utilize much lower priced foreign labor. And if some people think they have discovered a substitute for work, I want to leave them with this interesting thought . . .

The LEADERS and those who will be the future leaders in this country ARE WORKING TWELVE TO SIXTEEN HOURS A DAY!

Chapter 65

If You Would Control Others . . .

This chapter contains a magic word which, if you use it constantly, will enable you to exert substantial control over others. Some of the principal advantages of this magic word are that its use by you will greatly eliminate in others the debilitating effects of personal discouragement, disappointment, anxiety, depression and underachievement.

Also, it will eliminate those same unhappy, enervating feelings in yourself.

The magic word which will make it possible for you to perform such miracles is . . . HOPE!

You control people, through improving their total attitudes, when you give them hope. You lose your control over people—and lose your ability to help them—when you take away their hope.

What a powerful force HOPE is! Yet most people do not realize it and few people, indeed, make the most effective use of hope.

The negative side—the *lack of hope*—is undermining so many efforts which could be constructive that perhaps we should first consider some examples of what disastrous effects result from the lack or loss of hope.

From the individual's standpoint, probably the most devastating result of the loss of sustaining hope is alcoholism or drug addiction. When an individual feels certain that all hope for the future is gone, he or she tries to eliminate such an intolerable, hopeless future by fleeing reality—which emphasizes how vital it is that there always must be held out hope of something desirable in life. Just so there is HOPE, the expectation of a more desirable future.

Hope is so necessary that people will cling to the most improbable shred of it, rationalize it, even imagine it.

Hope is equally necessary in the control of groups, as it is in the control of individuals.

Let's consider the manipulation of hope in controlling the thinking, emotions and actions of the variously assorted groups of the under-privileged, under-educated, under-employed.

These groups' lack of hope of bettering their condition enables ambitious persons who would command positions of leadership among them to dramatize the groups' lack of hope. This is done individually, then in small meetings where emotions are stirred by emphasizing the unfairness of their past and present hopeless state, and finally in huge mass meetings where emotions are inflamed and hatreds directed toward the real or suspected cause of their hopelessness.

Demonstrations are organized to "call attention" to past and present injustices and inequalities, to warn of the groups' new awareness and resentment of discrimination, and to express increasing hostility toward the sources of their past and present hopeless conditions.

Finally, HOPE, emphasized by the emotionally-inflamed assurances of their leaders, becomes the motivation to action . . . to demands backed by threats and enforced by every hostile means from non-violent civil disturbance, disruption and disobedience . . . to riots, arson, vandalism, looting, killing . . . even to open rebellion —depending upon the character of the group and its leaders.

Such is the power of HOPE to provide the means of manipulating people—first, by dramatizing their *lack of hope*, then gradually offering *increasing hope*, and finally obtaining full control and motivation, even to the most extreme action, by *assuring the fulfillment of hope.*

This is not to imply that the offering of hope to the hopeless is bad—although some of the organized disruptions and violent, anti-social methods are. Indeed, having shown that the motivational power of hope unfortunately can lead to ruthless extremes, I want to emphasize that HOPE IS ONE OF THE GREATEST BENEFACTORS OF MANKIND.

Without HOPE . . . of some kind . . . for something . . . somewhere . . . sometime — I doubt that the human race could even continue to exist! Certainly, it would not progress.

There is no way to describe the scope and extent of hope, for hope is an essential ingredient of *everything* from a desired increase in pay . . . to the spiritual longing for eternal fellowship with God. Hope is IN everything. There are those who say that hope IS everything!

He who gives HOPE gives relief from discouragement, anxiety and depression. That, alone, is reason enough to give HOPE. But, he who gives HOPE, also gives motivation to strive for the results hoped for. Hope breaks the bonds of inertia and starts people toward achievement.

So, by all means, give HOPE to everyone who needs it! Give HOPE to all who need hope, giving it not as a means of exploiting them or organizing them for your selfish gains—but give HOPE to alleviate discouragement, anxiety and despair. Give HOPE to stimulate inspiration, to activate motivation and to spur achievement!

Having considered the effects of HOPE on individuals and groups, let's explore the tremendous encouragement of HOPE in the advancement of nations—and the dangers of *lack of* HOPE in international relations.

A nation is like a person. A nation is like a group. In fact, a nation simply is a composition of individuals and groups—and it reacts in much the same manner to hope or the lack of it. If we would make another nation our friend, we must offer that nation *hope* of achieving its national objectives through its friendship with us. And we must do it *convincingly.* Unfortunately, our nation, which has developed the art of selling (of *convincing*) to an exceptional degree, has been exceedingly unsuccessful in convincing other nations of its sincerity in providing them the hope—and, often to a substantial extent, the means—of attaining their national ambitions through their friendship with us. We need—desperately need—to do much better. Not by squandering our resources, but by establishing our credibility. Our nation needs to *prove*, not only its sincerity, but its *ability* to help fulfill the HOPE, the aspirations, of friendly nations.

And finally, what happens to a nation which *loses* HOPE? The same thing which happens to individuals and groups. Frustration! And frustration is a principal cause of aggression (see Chapter 12: "Frustration Causes Aggression"). If we are going to have less aggression—by nations, groups or individuals—then we are going to have to *replace frustration with* HOPE!

You can start . . . in your own life . . . and in your own way . . . by using the magic of HOPE . . . now!

Chapter 66

Make Progress...Or Stand Aside

This amazing life which each of us is privileged to live—is a life of many choices. Some of those choices determine the future course of our lives.

One of those future-determining choices is: "MAKE PROGRESS . . . or *stand aside!*"

It wisely has been said through the centuries, "The world makes way for those who make progress." So you have your choice of making progress or standing aside for those who do. Actually if you do not go forward, you not only must get out of the way of those who do, but you will fall behind farther and farther—into oblivion!

One only need look at the process of evolution to see that this need to *make continuous progress* is a requirement of survival. All living things—plant and animal—must first adjust to their environment, then improve (make progress) at a rate equal to, or preferably, better than, competing species. Otherwise they would be crowded out or, in some competitive manner, be exterminated by more progressive species. Nature demands progress.

Now let's change our focus from the eons of development to examine only the most recent fragment of time in man's process of evolution. There are several methods of doing this.

One method is to read what the best thinkers throughout history have written concerning their observations of progress—or the lack of it—as applied to their fellow men. In doing this, I have found agreement with the fact that the requirement to progress is a law of nature. Here are a few observations of the world's best thinkers:

"The true law is progress and development. Whenever civilization pauses in the march of conquest, it is overthrown", wrote William Gilmore Simms, the American author.

"Progress is the law of life", wrote Robert Browning.

"Nature knows no pause in progress and development, and attaches her curse on all inaction", wrote Goethe.

There you have the thoughts on progress as observed by three great, and very different, types of thinkers. You will find that the world's best thinkers agree with the idea that Goethe expressed best, "Nature knows no pause in progress and development." Here you have the often-restated concept that progress is a natural law. Then to continue Goethe's statement "(Nature) attaches her curse on all inaction." Or to restate it in the words of this chapter's heading, "Make progress . . . or stand aside."

Only you cannot just stand aside for long, because the penalty for inaction is oblivion—"nature's curse," as Goethe put it.

So we learn from nature's own law of evolution that we must either make progress or make way for those who do.

And we find that this also has been the observation of the great thinkers throughout history.

Now let's make it personal. What has been your own appraisal of the people you know who have been successful? Haven't these successful people always stood for progress? Haven't they always had a "progressive image"? Certain words always have been associated with success. "Progress" is one of them. So if *you* want to attract attention, get promoted, get elected, *get ahead* . . . then get a reputation for *making progress!*

How do you start making progress? There's a saying in the Navy that a Captain who waited until his ship was perfectly ready to go to sea, would never leave the dock. Progress is not perfection. Progress is moving forward. You don't have to be perfect. You *do* have to *progress!*

The path of progress consists of stepstones built of ideas, one after the other, leading always forward toward a distant horizon beyond which we cannot see—except the bright glow of a destiny worthy of our trip.

But suppose one of your stepstones is insecure—and you fall! You won't be the first to have fallen on the path of progress. Only the failures didn't get up. And the successes always fell *forward* . . . so when they got up they found that they had advanced by falling! That's one of the techniques of progress: FALL FORWARD!

There are so many techniques for making progress that it would require an entire book just to list them. The rewards are so great that you should spare neither time nor effort in making yourself a symbol of progress wherever you go.

The choice is yours *now* . . . either make progress—or make way for those who do.

The world will not remember, nor highly pay, those who stand aside.

Chapter 67

Stay In The Eye Of The Hurricane

A hurricane is a system of terrific winds rotating in a huge circle many miles in diameter. The force of the winds sometimes exceeds 100 miles an hour and results in great damage and destruction. With its accompanying deluge of rain, its flashing lightning and roaring thunder, a hurricane is a terrifying experience.

Except . . .

If you could stay in the center of the circle of whirling winds, in the "eye" of the hurricane, you would be in an area of great calm! And that is the point of this brief chapter. From time to time, you will experience the personal storms which are a natural—and, apparently, a necessary—part of each life. Sometimes these personal storms will be of hurricane velocity. They could destroy you physically, mentally, emotionally.

Unless . . .

Unless you can find the calm center of each personal storm—the "eye" of your own hurricane—and stay there, secure in the knowledge that there always is—and always will be—a place of peace in each personal disaster, if you will but seek it in the trust that, in every misfortune, nature provides a haven equal to your faith.

So in each personal hurricane in your life, do not panic. Stand firm in the center. Do not flee to the edges, because that's where the terrible winds are . . . and the thunder, the lightning, the deluge . . . and destruction.

There is danger and pain on the raw edge of trouble. Seek the center. For only in the center is there perfect stability, just as the exact center of a whirling wheel does not move.

It takes courage and faith to go to the center of a hurricane—or a personal problem.

But then it is only through courage and faith that we find calm and peace in a troubled world.

Chapter 68

How Important Is It To You?

There is an old fable concerning a dog that bragged about his speed as a runner. One day the dog chased a rabbit but failed to catch it. Other dogs made fun of him but he explained, "Remember the rabbit was running for his life, while I was running only for the fun of chasing him".

In that fable you will find one of the most valuable lessons for success in life. It simply is this:

A key factor in success is how *hard* you really try. And how *hard* you try depends upon how *important* it is to *you!*

In Chapter 55, titled: "How To Be A Billionnaire", I gave you billionaire J. Paul Getty's advice on how to do it: "TRY HARDER!"

Well, how does one develop the personal drive to try harder?

You'll find the key in one word: DESIRE.

And *desire* depends upon how *important* it is to *you!*

In the fable just told, we learned that the dog did not catch the fleeing rabbit because the dog was merely chasing the rabbit for fun. Catching the rabbit was *not important* to the dog. But whether or not he got caught, *was important* to the rabbit! It was a matter of life or death!

You could foretell the result. The rabbit *tried harder!* It was more important to *him*!

And you can sum it up in one word: DESIRE! Every achievement begins with desire. Have you thoughtfully considered the power of *desire*? Do you know that *desire* will get you just about *anything* you want in life?

William James, probably the greatest thinker of modern times, wrote: "If you only care *enough* for the result, you will almost certainly attain it. If you wish to be rich, you will be rich; if you wish to be learned, you will be learned; if you wish to be good, you will be good. Only you must *really* wish these things."

There's the secret of getting what you want! You must "*care enough*" . . . you must "*really* wish"! You must have *desire!* And it must be a white-hot desire that burns itself into your subconscious, that sears its brand on your every thought and action, that becomes an overwhelming obession!

It has to be THAT IMPORTANT TO YOU!

Chapter 69

When There Were No Letters To Santa Claus

It was the month before Christmas . . . the week before Christmas . . . even the day before Christmas—and tiny fingers of tiny tots clumsily grasped their over-sized pencils and scribbled, marked or crudely drew, "Dear Santa, please bring me . . ."

So many letters! Asking for so many things! Some were just a series of marks, but their little writers knew what they meant—and they knew Santa could read them, too. Some were more legible, painstakingly and largely drawn, even if the lines of letters were a bit diagonal.

Most of the letters said, "Please," somewhere. Some merely said, "I want . . . ", and some were downright demanding: "Bring me this . . . and bring me that." You could almost read the personalities of the parents in the manner of asking they had taught their children, just as you can read the character of the parents in the actions of their children (a statement which the parents of some children would like to disclaim and probably will).

But about those letters to Santa Claus: all of them, in whatever manner, *asked* for things. And that's good! In fact, the writing of letters to the jolly old man with white beard and red suit is part of the fun of Christmastime, not only for little children, but for their parents, too, who must have been made a little nobler to have touched such trusting faith.

So what's wrong?

What's wrong—what's so very wrong—is that *after* the gifts had been received, there were NO letters to Santa Claus, saying, "Dear Santa, THANK YOU . . . "

Before Christmas, perhaps a million letters, saying, "I *want*" . . . "*bring me*"—but after the gifts were received, *no* letters (or just a few) saying, "THANK YOU"!

We cannot blame the little children. They can only learn what they are taught.

But we can pause to consider what kind of world we adults have built—where most of the emphasis is on "*I want*" and almost none on appreciation and gratitude. And what kind of world are we building for the future? For it is trite but true, that as the twig is bent, so is the tree.

Which reminds me . . . I recently asked a very busy and important business executive to do me a personal favor. It meant nothing to him but time-consuming inconvenience, but it was urgent and important to me—and I emphasized the urgency to such an extent that I received, the very next morning, the documents I requested. I used them at once, then turned my interest to other matters.

It wasn't until four days later that I realized with shocked embarrassment that I had been so preoccupied with using what he had sent me, that I hadn't even thought to thank my benefactor!

As the twig is bent . . .

I wish I had been taught to write "THANK YOU" letters to Santa Claus!

Were YOU?

Chapter 70

Are You Chicken Or Eagle?

A little boy who lived in the mountains found an eagle's nest in a tree high on a rocky crag. In the nest was an eagle's egg. The boy took the egg home and placed it in a hen's nest under a setting hen. After being placed under a succession of setting hens, the eagle's egg finally hatched, along with the chicken eggs.

The baby eaglet played with the baby chicks and of course thought he was just like them—a chicken.

Since the eaglet *believed* he was a chicken he, of course, lived and acted like a chicken. He did not try to fly, but remained with the chickens in the fenced-in chicken yard. Yet, as the eagle grew bigger and stronger, there came a realization inside him that made him feel that he was more than a chicken—he felt the urge to fly. After a few tries, the eagle began to *believe* he really could fly.

And because he *believed* he could—he *could*!

So he stretched his mighty wings and began to fly . . . higher . . . higher . . . higher . . . until he reached his new home on top of a lofty mountain. Because he *believed* in a greater destiny, he knew he was not a chicken, confined to a dirty chicken yard. Because he *believed*—his belief released his real powers. He now lived on the highest pinnacle and soared through the bright, blue sky as the proud symbol of courage and freedom—the American Eagle!

The most powerful forces of nature are the *invisible* ones: heat, sound, wind, electricity, gravity—just as the most powerful forces of man also are invisible: love, thought, desire, *belief*.

In the foregoing story, as long as the eagle *believed* he was a chicken, he lived and acted like a chicken. Insofar as the eagle was concerned, he *was* what he believed—a chicken. But just as soon as the eagle began to *believe* he had powers and capabilities greater than a chicken, his powers and capabilities increased to equal his *belief!*

And so you can increase you own powers and capabilities to the exact extent that you increase your *belief* in them. Psychologists tell us that: "Whatever the mind can conceive and *believe,* man can achieve. "The Bible said it much earlier: "ALL things are possible for him that *believeth*."

Not only can you achieve in direct proportion to your beliefs, you *actually become* what you *believe!*

The Bible says: "As a man thinketh in his heart (*deeply believes*), *so is he*."

Buddha taught: "ALL that we *are* is the result of what we have thought (*deeply believed*)."

Throughout the teachings of all great religions, all great thinkers, all great philosophers, and now, modern psychologists, are these two monumental facts: (1) You can *achieve* whatever you *believe* you can, and (2) you *are* the result of your *beliefs.*

ALL the great thinkers throughout history, up to and including modern times, cannot *all* be wrong!

William James, famed philosopher and psychologist of Harvard, taught: *"Belief creates the actual fact."*

Emerson, one of the wisest men this nation has ever produced, wrote: "No accomplishment, no assistance, no training, can compensate for lack of *belief.*"

As famed author Bruce Barton said: "Nothing splendid has even been achieved except by those who dared *believe* that something inside them was superior to circumstance."

What do YOU dare BELIEVE?

Are you CHICKEN or EAGLE?

Chapter 71

Who Changes The Water?

Some people say that humanity is like a colony of ants on a burning log floating down a broad river. Even as the log approaches a cataclysmic waterfall, the ants argue among themselves about who is the pilot.

Other people say that life is like a candle. It is lighted at birth and henceforth sheds its dim light upon its limited surroundings, flickering uncertainly in every breeze, knowing that any sudden gust of wind will extinguish it, and, finally, futilely sputtering out as the tallow is consumed.

Of course, just saying life is like a candle does not make it so. And there still would remain two relevant questions. Who lit the candle? And, why?

There are other considerations.

It wisely has been said that an undevout astronomer is an idiot.

To be an atheist, one would have to conceive

effects with no cause, motion without a mover, a circle without a center, time without eternity.

To be an atheist, one would have to conceive a second without a first, action without energy, thought without a thinker, a thing formed from nothing by nothing.

To be an atheist, one would have to believe that what is made, exists, but that which made it does not exist. Try applying that proposition to the infinity of the universe!

Such beliefs are so against natural reason as to be untenable to any sane mind.

But they were the subject of a serious discussion between two goldfish as they swam in their crystal-clear bowl. Finally, one goldfish in exasperation concluded the argument with this pertinent question, "*So . . . if there isn't a God, who changes the water?*"

Chapter 72

The Pumpkin Shaped Like A Jug

A farmer exhibited at a county fair a pumpkin in the exact shape of a two-gallon jug.

This unusually-shaped pumpkin caused quite a lot of comment and, of course, the farmer was asked how he accomplished it. "When the pumpkin was no bigger than my thumb," he explained, "I stuck it in a glass jug and just let it grow. When it filled the jug, it quit growing."

What the walls of the jug did to the pumpkin, our plans do to us. Our plans shape—and limit—our lives, just as the jug limited the pumpkin. We can never be bigger than our plans.

As one of the master strategists of life admonished, "Make no little plans!"

Place no limit, no restriction, on your goals in life. MAKE no little plans! And do not let others, for whatever purpose, limit your goals. ACCEPT no little plans! For your plans will shape—and limit—your life just as surely as the size and shape of the jug shaped and limited the size of the pumpkin.

It is better to be a man of small abilities with a big plan, than to be a man of great abilities with a small plan.

If you would be a leader, know this: People will not follow a leader who cannot tell them where he is going and who cannot show them a feasible plan for getting there.

Without a step-by-step plan, you cannot judge progress. If you cannot show progress, you cannot prove achievement. If you cannot prove achievement, you cannot inspire enthusiasm. And if you cannot inspire enthusiasm—who needs you?

If you would be a leader, you must point to a worthy goal—to a Promised Land. And so we recall that great old story of Moses, leading his people for forty years through the wilderness to the Promised Land. His people followed him for forty years, because beyond the wilderness, Moses had a goal and always he pointed toward it. He taught the lesson which is eternally true for every great leader—he must point to a Promised Land!

Yes, you must have a worthy goal. And to reach that goal you must have a plan. But, like the pumpkin at the beginning of this chapter, the size of your plan will determine the size of your future.

How big a pumpkin will you be?

Chapter 73

Pressure Creates Resistance

As the real pros in influencing people know: PRESSURE CREATES RESISTANCE.

It seems incredible that the novices haven't learned. Yet they persist in bringing pressure on the people whose good will they must have in order to succeed. And pressure inevitably creates resistance—in physics, in psychology, in politics, in salesmanship, in civil rights militancy, in war, in every relationship involving people.

Certainly, if you possess overwhelming power, you can impose your will. But you may live to regret it. (Many people have not lived that long!)

The surest way to increase resistance is to apply pressure. And the more obvious the pressure, the more open and hostile the resistance.

Consider the civil rights militants. The gains supposedly won by pressure—by riots, disruption, violent demonstrations—were illusionary. They filled a frustrated need for recognition. They gratified the egos of some ambitious leaders and gave means of venting the justified resentment of their followers. But from the practical standpoint of permanently achieving the ultimate objective of an unquestionably just cause, they did their cause much more harm than good. They created more resistance—which, although invisible, will exist for years—than they achieved progress, even through the illusion of intimidation and capitulation may (or may not) have seemed to result from the pressure.

To put it very simply, one cannot throw a rock through a window in a quiet, peaceful neighborhood and then ring the doorbell and say, "I just wanted you to know what a good neighbor I would be."

Yet activities all too similar, and on ominously massive scales, have been used to "call attention" as some civil rights leaders put it. But to "call attention" in a way that arouses resentment, creates resistance, and worse, is hardly the way to win welcome and subsequent friendship.

If people would only realize that PRESSURE CREATES RESISTANCE, how much more pleasantly, justly and successfully, differences could be resolved.

Even between nations.

We never seem to learn from history—especially our own history! Way back about seventy years ago, we got involved in a "little war" half way around the world, in the Philippines. From our great superiority of power, we felt all we had to do was apply "pressure". But the more pressure we applied, the more resistance we encountered. So we sent 20,000 U. S. troops. They were matched by equal resistance.

Our General Elwell S. Otis announced that to win the war we really needed 30,000 troops. But the more pressure, the more resistance. The more Filipinos we killed, the more took their places.

President McKinley denounced the critics and sent 40,000 troops. Then 50,000. Then 60,000. Finally the "pressure" required to meet the "resistance" of what started out to be a few ragged Filipinos in a then-undeveloped country rose to a call for 100,000 U. S. troops.

Any similarity between this "little Asian war" and Vietnam . . . is purely a matter of history.

We learn some of our hardest lessons from history—only we seem to have to keep learning them over and over again.

Now, to simpler, everyday lessons on our subject that PRESSURE CREATES RESISTANCE. Every salesman knows—or should know—that. And every buyer will confirm it. Everyone who has sought to train a child, or to influence a husband or wife knows it—or soon finds it out!

It is so fundamental a principle of psychology that it should need no repeating here. But having read today's newspaper, the lessons of the news impel me to re-emphasize . . .

PRESSURE CREATES RESISTANCE! ! !

Chapter 74

The Happiness (?) Of Doing Without

There is a philosophy which teaches that we can eliminate our needs by eliminating their causes. So we can. For example, we can eliminate our need for shoes by cutting off our feet.

But I do not want to make light of this philosophy by citing extreme examples. Indeed, there is considerable merit to it—not in the extreme of cutting off our feet—but in our moderation of desire, in our restraint of acquisition.

When I was a very young man, I read a little book entitled, "The Tyranny Of Things." It taught a common-sense lesson which I failed to heed, and I'm not sure I should have heeded it anyway. But since it is an unavoidable problem for each of us, let's face up to it, this tyranny of things.

Let's first examine, briefly, the case for simplifying our lives by disdaining the abundance which is so lavishly spread before us. We have merely to discipline ourselves against desire; seek and be satisfied with the bare necessities. For many this wouid be small accomplishment. And we would have to define our terms. What are "bare necessities" today? The possessions which were considered luxuries not too long ago, now are considered necessities by millions.

However, many of the great religions and philosophies of the world have taught the shunning of all worldly goods. The lives of great thinkers have emphasized their complete freedom from this "tyranny of things". Barefoot Socrates, Christ with only the clothes He wore, Ghandi with only his loin cloth and dollar watch, Thoreau in his self-built cabin at Walden—and the examples could be almost endless.

Certainly, I am not one who can argue with such great thinkers, their religions and philosophies. Their influence has stood the test of history. I can only suggest that there may be other interpretations.

When Thoreau writes, "Money is not required to buy one necessity of the soul," I cannot debate that. I can only suggest that this philosophy of doing without puts unnecessary limits on living. I do not say that deprivation is wrong; I merely say that it is a discipline which is desirable in its most extreme forms only to a very few who seek supreme sacrifice as a means to spiritual—and in some cases, mental—power. Or, for those who are unwilling to provide the effort necessary to obtain more than bare essentials, so that their activities can be used elsewhere.

But for the rest of us, what's wrong with rightly having a share of the vast abundance which nature (or

God, if you prefer) continues to make so profusely available to those whom nature (or God) has given both the desire for, and the ability to obtain?

Otherwise, why are we given the desire? Why are we given the ability? Why the abundance? If life, through an incomprehensible and magnificent process, spreads before us a table overflowing with abundance, shall we turn aside and let the gifts of nature rot? Is there not a purpose in the providing? Otherwise why are things for our use provided, if we are not to accept them?

Perhaps examples are better than general questions.

Is the little poor girl, looking wistfully at the doll in the store window, somehow better by not having the doll? Is her character strengthened by doing without—or would it be better if she could own and cuddle the doll in her tiny arms, expressing the child-mother love which only little girls can give their dolls? Would she receive more happiness by doing without? Or even more character?

Are the backward, starving millions of India better in any way than the progressive, affluent Americans? Granting the many moral, spiritual and other deficiencies of our affluent society, is it not better for us to accept our blessings, to multiply them, and to share them with the less fortunate? Or must we seek, instead, the moral discipline of doing without?

Certainly there is more than one philosophy—so why not a Philosophy of Abundance? Surely there is more than one interpretation of a religion which sometimes seems to advocate the doing without all worldly things—when the God of that same religion provides an abundance far surpassing the needs of all mankind so, perhaps instead of doing without, we should seek the will and the wisdom for the distribution of that abundance to all needy peoples throughout the world.

Why not a Philosophy of Abundance? Why not the *full* utilization of world resources: land, people, education, finance, transportation—to the end that all mankind shall live in abundance, so that no man (or nation) need covet that which is his neighbor's, and there shall be neither need nor greed, thus establishing the foundation for peace on earth and goodwill among men.

Chapter 75

The Ignorant Are The Most Violent

Several centuries ago, wise Alexander Pope wrote a simple statement of fact which offers benefits in many phases of modern conduct.

Pope wrote, "There never was any party, faction or sect, in which the most ignorant were not the most violent."

It should be a deterrent to violence—or to the advocacy of violence—just for it to be widely known that violence would publicly and privately brand an individual or group as being the "most ignorant" of their fellow men.

It will better prepare us to deal with violence, by knowing that it will come from the most ignorant.

And it should motivate us, not only to speed, but to spread, education to all levels of our society, knowing that by increasing education we proportionately diminsh one of the major causes of violence.

But let us note carefully the part education plays in violence. Often educated leaders use their own knowledge to arouse the violence of more ignorant followers. A leader, who will choose the road of violence also will choose the most ignorant to carry out his purpose.

In all of the major revolutions and rebellions throughout history, the leadership came from the educated, but the violent, mass manpower came from the most ignorant.

As education increases in quality and is spread throughout all populations, there will be a marked decrease in the use of violence in problem-solving. And, as you progress through life, you learn that problem-solving is "the name of the game".

There are better ways of solving problems—personal, group, national and international—than by introducing violence or even the threat of violence. Surely, by now, we have sufficient evidence to prove that.

In a recent chapter (Chapter 73: "Pressure Creates Resistance") it was pointed out that applying various forms of pressure actually produced the opposite of the result hoped for. Instead of causing acquiescence, retreat or collapse, pressure actually creates resistance in exact proportion to the degree of pressure applied.

Since violence is an extreme form of pressure, violence and even the threat of violence creates resistance. And being an extreme form of pressure, violence creates extreme forms of resistance: hostility and counter-violence. Also, violence and threats of violence have a built-in tendency to escalate. Thus, violence breeds increasing violence.

How do we stop it?

Simply by going back to our original premise: "The ignorant are the most violent." We must eliminate ignorance by education. And we must do it soon—because the forms of violence, now available, already are capable of exterminating us.

And the first thing we must teach is that the use or threat of violence is an admission of ignorance.

Will those who want to admit that they are ignorant, please step forward . . .

Chapter 76

The Magic Word That Changes Things

There is a magic little word.

It has the power to change things from bad to good.

Or, from good to bad.

It depends upon how you use this magic little word.

You always are in full control of its use, so you have the power to change bad to good, to change unhappiness into happiness, to change failure into success, to work miracles in your life and in the lives of others—by the use of this magic little word.

Here is unexpected power which you may not have realized you had—or how to use it! So let's try!

The magic little word which has the power to change things is . . . "BUT."

So you don't believe that such an ordinary little word as "BUT" contains the magic power to change things? To work miracles of happiness and success?

Here's proof!

Suppose you have lost your job. You say, "Yes, I have lost my job . . . BUT . . . this releases me to devote my full time to finding a better job for which I am better qualified. I might never have had the courage to quit and thus would have spent my life in a rut . . . BUT . . . now I am free to discover what I really want to do in life and get a job which is satisfying as well as more rewarding."

Note that the little word "BUT" makes the transition from the negative to the positive, from bad to good.

Suppose you have lost someone very near and dear to you. You say, "Yes, it is a heartbreaking tragedy . . . BUT . . . I shall *admit* it is *so* and cannot be otherwise, I shall *accept* what cannot be changed, I shall *adapt* my life to what I have *accepted* as reality and I shall by positive *action* lose myself in a cause which is so much bigger than I am that it also is bigger than anything which has happened to me."

Note, again, that it is the little word "BUT" which makes the transition from the negative to the positive, from tragedy to acceptance and then to self-submerging action.

Suppose the life goal for which you have studied, worked and sacrificed, suddenly is snatched from your grasp and dashed to pieces on the hard rocks of fate. You say, "Yes, *that* goal is lost . . . BUT . . . it is a Law of Life that when Fate closes one door, Faith opens another, so I shall seek the open door and discover a greater goal—and achieve it!

Again, the magic little word "BUT" has changed the negative into the positive, the bad into good.

And example could follow example. It is time now to state the formula so that it can be visualized and memorized to become a conditioned reflex which automatically will use the magic word "BUT" to make the transition from the negative to the positive, and change bad into good—in *your* life.

The formula (or call it a method or technique, if you prefer) simply is this:

(1) Whenever *anything* bad happens, immediately *admit* it (never play make-believe with trouble) and *verbalize* it, either by describing it aloud or silently to yourself. The purpose is to get it stated clearly so that you know *exactly* what bad condition you want to change.

(2) Then having mentally and verbally defined the bad condition (the negative) which you want to change, *emphasize with total concentration* the transforming word . . . "BUT."

(3) Follow the transition word "BUT" with the *positive affirmation* that you will transform the bad condition into the best possible situation—and *begin at once* to do so.

Now let's try it on another example: Suppose you have lost a substantial amount of money in an ill-conceived business venture.

(1) Admit and verbalize the bad condition thus: "Yes, I have lost a lot of money . . .

(2) Then apply the transforming power of the magic word "BUT" so that your statement now is: "Yes, I have lost a lot of money . . . BUT . . ."

(3) Finally, follow "BUT" with a *positive affirmation put into effect immediately by action:* "the knowledge and experience I have gained will enable me to earn much more money than I lost, and I shall begin to do so at once!"

So there you have the Magic Word "BUT" Formula in action: "Yes, I have lost a lot of money (*negative*) . . . BUT . . . (*transformation*) . . . the knowledge and experience I have gained will enable me to earn much more money than I lost, and I shall begin to do so at once!" (*positive affirmation put into effect immediately by action*).

Whenever something bad happens, *always* apply the magic word "BUT" to transform bad to good.

It's a revolutionary idea—*which may revolutionize your life!*

Chapter 77

Are You Overwhelmed?

One of the greatest disasters of life is to be overwhelmed by it.

The depressing feeling that you are overburdened beyond your capacity to cope with life's problems and responsibilities is one of the most painful of all emotions. Unlike many painful emotions which come as sudden shocks and are soon over, the depression of being overwhelmed is one that endures, and feeds on itself to grow into an increasingly greater burden.

When life's burdens completely overwhelm the victim, the result is insanity in one of its most tragic forms. Or often suicide.

Why should this be, this permitting ourselves to be overwhelmed? Life does not impose on anyone burdens beyond his capacitity to bear. Whatever our burdens, we are given the strength to bear them. But like the frenzied swimmer in water he does not realize is shallow, we panic and drown—when all we need to do is stand up.

Just knowing it is in the nature of life that we are equal to our tasks, often removes our panic and we stand up, head above the swirling waters which, moments before, we thought would submerge us.

The depression of being overwhelmed by the burdens of life is self-imposed or imposed by others. It is something we do to ourselves or that we permit others to do to us.

How do we prevent it?

First, know that—no matter how great your burdens may be, you are given the strength to carry them. You have an inner strength equal to the task.

Second, simplify. Do not permit yourself to become entangled in too many of the complexities of a universe which is far too complicated for any person to understand, much less manage, even an infinitesimal part of it. Be willing to accept a satisfying personal involvement in it—and let the rest of it alone. Nobody appointed you Manager of the World and it may reassure you to know how few people really are depending on you to solve the world's problems.

You will, however, find many people who will seek to unload their problems on you or, in many presumptious ways, add additional problems to those you already have. So do as recommended in Chapter 19: push your wheelbarrow upside down, or people will throw all kinds of things into it. Be content to solve your own problems and be very, very selective about additional burdens you add to your own load.

Sufficient unto each day are the burdens thereof. The problems of yesterday, added to the anticipated problems of tomorrow, and all piled upon the burden you are carrying today, will make the strongest falter. Live one day at a time. Better still, live one hour, even one minute, at a time. Certainly, cope with only one problem at a time. Shut out of your life all the unpleasant yesterdays and all the frightening, uncertain tomorrows. Shut out, temporarily, all of today—except just one problem—and you will find the one problem, not overwhelming, but stimulating.

Then you will get enjoyment from life for what it really is: a problem-solving adventure!

Divide and conquer, as recommended in Chapter 2. That's the way to handle a difficult problem. Divide each problem into its smallest parts, then methodically solve each part, one at a time. Start with the easiest part first, so you will be sure to succeed in solving that. This will start the momentum of achievement, the continuous thrill of consecutive successes!

Throw away your problem-magnifying-glass! Quit making mountains out of molehills—and start making molehills out of mountains!

Then, instead of being overwhelmed by the burdens of life—you will overwhelm them!

The difference is . . . happiness!

Chapter 78

The Birds Which Had No Wings

If you think you have a burden, just remember the beautiful and inspiring story which Schiller, the German author, loved to tell the children:

"Once upon a time, the birds had no wings. They crawled about the earth. Then one day God threw wings at their feet and commanded them to pick up the wings and carry them on their backs. At first, it seemed very hard. The little birds didn't want to carry those heavy, unwieldy wings. But they loved the Lord and, in obedience, they picked up the wings and carried them on their backs.

"And, lo, the wings fastened there! What they once had thought was a hampering weight and a burden, enabled them to fly!"

It is one of the great lessons of life, that the burdens we carry by necessity or by choice—instead of weighting us down, actually can lift us up!

There is no escaping the burdens of life because, indeed, they are a part of life, itself. Our joy in living the brief span of time allotted us, is in our attitude toward our burdens, in the very manner in which we accept and carry them.

We might learn our lesson from those hardy souls who, throughout history, have been forced in slavery or servitude, to handle physical burdens almost beyond endurance. We think of those muscled oarsmen who pulled the oars of ancient ships when there was no wind to fill the sails. And the Negro slaves who pulled the barges along the Mississippi before Robert Fulton's steamboats plied the waterways and spared their backs for bales of cotton. And, we remember, because of their stirring song, the Volga boatmen.

What did they do when their physical burdens became almost unbearable?

They sang!

So, once again, we come to that omnipotent word (which, no matter how hard your author tries to avoid repetition, still keeps recurring) . . . ACCEPTANCE!

No matter what burdens life places upon you, or you choose to carry for someone else—*accept* them . . . and *sing!*

It is a psychological fact—which was known to the ancients long before there were psychologists—that if you *accept* your burdens with the attitude of progressing forward, with a song on your lips, or at least in your heart, then your burdens become, by some miracle of nature, much lighter . . . so much lighter that they may spiritually lift you up!

And, like the heavy wings which were given the little birds to carry on their backs, but which became attached so birds could fly, your burdens may have been given you for the very purpose of lifting you above the humdrum—to spiritual heights!

Just one of Schiller's fairy tales?

Or one of the paradoxes of which a rewarding life is built?

You'll never know until you try.

Chapter 79

Let It Rain

There is a great wisdom in a simple, little statement by Longfellow in *Tales of A Wayside Inn:*

"For after all, the best thing one can do when it is raining, is to let it rain."

And so we should—because we must.

Perhaps that is the greatest lesson of this book.

Although its 80 chapters were written to give readers a wide variety of stimulating and rewarding THOUGHTS TO BUILD ON, and each chapter was planned to be entirely different from and unrelated to all other chapters, yet as we near its end and review its thoughts, there seems to be one predominantly recurring lesson which applies to many of the life situations with which this book deals.

It is the philosophy of ACCEPTING what cannot be changed.

It is the psychology of acceptance of the inevitable. It is being willing to have it so, if it cannot be otherwise.

There are so many circumstances and events of life which we can neither understand nor change. We are bewildered by the unevenhandedness of fate and become suspicious that its dice are loaded as we daily roll them in the game of life.

Yet the universe of which we are such a minuscule part is, itself, infinitely perfect precision and balance. The knowledge that we are a part of such infinite perfection should provide foundation for our faith.

And it is in that environment of eternal and absolute perfection that we must realize our being—and accept that which we cannot change, and often do not understand.

Because, it is only through acceptance that we can transcend the inevitable difficulties and tragedies which otherwise would wreck us.

Let us be pragmatic, if we must, and submit to acceptance of what cannot be changed, because that is the only way to peace of mind and spirit in a troubled world.

But if we can, let us do better than just be pragmatic. Let us, through faith that exceeds understanding, place our acceptance on the altar of Infinity, not as a sacrifice, but as a token of belief.

Having found the means, through acceptance, of transcending difficulties and tragedies which inevitably are a part of life, having assured ourselves of survival from the shipwreck of sudden storms—let us now seek the abundance of good things, good times and good deeds which are the unlimited rewards for our having acquired the inner resources to surmount adversity.

Let us remember the lesson of previous chapters, that when Fate closes one door, Faith opens another—so that we may move on to a greater goal and achieve our highest destiny.

Chapter 80

Not By Bread Alone

So now we have come full circle. Your author began this book by quoting from the Bible, "As a man *thinketh* . . . so *is* he."

Then from Buddha, "ALL that we *are* is the result of what we have *thought*."

And from William James, "Belief (*thought*) creates the *actual fact*."

This entire book could have been written nailing proof upon evidence—that WE BECOME WHAT WE THINK.

Just as the kind of food we eat builds our bodies, so the thoughts we think build our characters—what we really are or subsequently will become.

So what should we think about?

Surely we should think more and better thoughts than are given in this book. This book is intended to be only a tempting beginning in the field of thought—a sort of thought-starter, nothing more.

The thoughts—or beginnings of thoughts—contained in this book are deliberately incomplete and, hopefully, provocative as you continue along each partial thought-path.

This is a book of THOUGHTS TO BUILD ON. It is not intended to do your thinking for you.

Each brief chapter has brought you a different thought—or, at least, a different viewpoint on an idea which is so interwoven in life that it insists on re-occurring. Thus, each chapter has been totally unrelated to the preceding and following chapters. You can read this book forward, backward, start in the middle or anywhere. You are set free to ponder each thought briefly . . . or pass it by . . . or think about it as deeply and as long as you wish.

No effort has been made to win your agreement. In fact, your disagreement would be welcomed as evidence that this book has accomplished its purpose of stimulating thought.

While this is a chair-side book, and its author hopes you will keep it there when it is not otherwise in use, it can be used to rewardingly fill those brief empty spaces of time too often wasted idly, while you are commuting or waiting.

It will give you an unlimited variety of THOUGHTS TO BUILD ON . . . and give you plenty of room to do your own thinking.

For . . . "As a man THINKETH—so IS he."